How to Write

Blockbuster

Sales Letters

BENJAMIN HART

DIRECTMAILCOPYWRITERS.COM

Outskirts Press, Inc.
Denver, Colorado

How to Write Blockbuster Sales Letters
All Rights Reserved
Copyright © 2006 Benjamin Hart

Outskirts Press
http://www.outskirtspress.com

ISBN-10: 1-59800-262-7
ISBN-13: 978-1-59800-262-1

Outskirts Press and the "OP" logo are trademarks belonging to Outskirts Press, Inc.

Printed in the United States of America

Contents

Chapter One
Selling

All of us spend much of our lives selling.

We are trying to sell not just tangible commercial products. We are also always selling our ideas and ourselves. We make every effort to sell our children on why they should act correctly and work hard in school.

We sell our wives on why we must stay late at the office or go on that hunting trip with the guys. We sell our boss on why our idea is best and why the company should follow our recommendations.

Selling is the science and art of persuasion—specifically, persuading others to do what you want them to do.

This book will help anyone and everyone who wants to be better at selling their products, themselves, or their ideas.

But most specifically, this book is about how to write and mail letters that will persuade people to buy your product or service.

If you follow the principles outlined in this book, you will be able to use direct mail successfully to grow your business immediately and perhaps even explosively.

My direct mail marketing letters have generated hundreds of millions of dollars in sales and donations for scores of businesses, non-profit organizations and political candidates over the years.

This book is jam packed with rules, laws, maxims, principles, concepts, precepts, commandments and case studies on how to write, create, and mail successful sales and lead generation letters—whether aimed at mass-market consumers or executives of major corporations.

Chapter Two
The two most important rules in this entire book

Here are the two most important rules in this entire book, and I'm putting them here for you, right on the second page of this book.

> *First, write about what your readers are interested in, not what you are interested in.*

Your readers do not care one wit about your business or who you are. They don't care about how hard you work or the fact that you've been in business since 1960. They don't care whether you are making money or losing money. They don't care what the names of your kids are or whether you are a really nice person. All they really care about is whether you can deliver what they want.

Do buyers care how much money Johnson and Johnson has spent to develop Tylenol?

Nope.

Do they care whether Johnson and Johnson is a big company, or even that it's reputable?

Nope.

Buyers of Tylenol only want to know: "Will this product make my headache go away, and make it go away now?"

> *And second, even if you are mailing to a million people, a successful sales letter must look, feel, and read like a personal communication from one person to another.*

Otherwise, your sales letter will just look like all the other junk mail that shows up in our mailboxes.

If your friend were to come to your home in person and present a business opportunity, you would listen. If an eight-year old girl knocks on your door and asks you to buy her Girl Scout cookies, you buy.

You are far more likely to buy from someone you talk with face-to-face than by answering a piece of junk mail that's obviously mass-produced. Rarely is anyone hired for a job based on his or her resume. A one-on-one personal interview is almost always required.

As much as possible, your letter must strive to capture a sense of one person standing in someone's kitchen having a conversation.

Okay, I guess you can stop reading. Because I've just given you the two key secrets of successful direct mail marketing.

If you remember nothing else, remember these two rules.

I know. This sounds pretty easy, which leads me to my next point...

Successful sales letter writing is as easy as golf

...which is why you should keep reading.

Direct mail sales letter writing looks so easy to the casual observer: Short staccato sentences written at a sixth grade level.

Direct mail sales letter writing looks like something almost anyone can do.

Of course, swinging a golf club at a stationary ball looks easy, too. Only someone who's tried hitting that blasted little ball straight and consistently knows how truly difficult it is.

Successful sales letter writing is very difficult.

It requires years of study and practice. And you can only learn it by actually doing it and seeing for yourself through trial and error what works and what doesn't work.

Golf is an impossible game to completely master, which is the reason people love it.

But golf is also playable by the average person. It's not like downhill ski racing where you'll kill yourself if you don't know what you're doing. Golf does not require great strength, speed, or athletic talent. It's a game anyone can play at a decent level if they take the time to learn the basics. Not like Tiger Woods, perhaps, but just about anyone can learn to be pretty darn good.

The same is true for writing successful sales letters.

You don't need to be a great writer to be successful.

You just need to know the basic fundamentals, and you can go out there in the marketplace and do just fine.

Chapter Three
Think "inside" the box

Everyone **is told** to "think outside the box."

Kids are told to "think outside the box." Employees are told by their bosses to "think outside the box." Advertising copywriters are told to "think outside the box."

I say the opposite. "Think inside the box."

Tiger Woods is not a great golfer because he has an *original* golf swing. Sure, if you look closely, there are some differences between his golf swing and that of Jack Nicklaus, Ben Hogan, or Bobby Jones. Most of these differences have to do with the way these men are built. But basically they all hit the ball about the same way. They all have sound fundamentals.

These men are the greatest golfers of all time because they mastered the basic fundamentals of golf better than their competitors—not all the time, but most of the time.

The same holds true for direct mail marketing.

Like golf, direct mail is very humbling. In golf I can occasionally hit as great a shot as Tiger Woods. And just when I think I'm starting to master the game, suddenly, and seemingly inexplicably, I find I can't hit the ball anymore at all. I'm back to playing my usual game.

I'm then forced to go back to the pro for another lesson to find out what the problem is.

Even Tiger Woods needs a teacher to keep his swing on track, to make sure he's not veering off course in some subtle way, to make sure his fundamentals are sound.

The same is true for the writer of sales letters.

You can write a blockbuster letter that breaks the bank with orders one day. And then, just when you think you've figured out the game and can't fail, your next letter crashes. And it's not always apparent exactly why it crashed.

I mean, I wouldn't have written the letter and spent all that money to mail it if I thought it was a bad letter.

If one of my packages flop, I'll give a copy to my copywriting peers and ask for their assessment of what went wrong with my letter. We'll do an autopsy. We'll analyze every aspect of the package. We'll

How To Write...

look at what lists we mailed. We'll see if there were mistakes in the way the package was assembled and produced. We'll usually come up with an answer, or at least a theory for why the letter failed.

Almost always the reason for a package performing poorly is that the writer has made some fundamental mistake, violated some basic marketing principle tied to the iron laws of human nature.

To be the biggest and most successful you usually have to be the first. But I prefer not to be the first because to be the first to market with a new idea is incredibly risky. Coke is #1 because it came first. Pepsi came second, so it will always be #2. But it's not bad being Pepsi.

No one could have predicted the success of Coke. But once Coke proved successful, this paved the way for competitors such as Pepsi, RC Cola, and so on.

I prefer not to be the first to do anything. I would rather watch others and see what's working and then follow in their wake. Maybe I'll try to do it a little better and make some refinements. But I'm very happy to watch others spend their money blazing new trails. Most of the trailblazers will fail.

A few will succeed. I will then learn from them. I will copy what they are doing. I will be very happy being #2, #3, or #4. And I will have taken far less risk. I'm not much of a gambler. Avis will always be the #2 car rental company behind Hertz. But it's not bad being Avis.

I'm happy to follow along behind the pioneers. I'm not interested in being Lewis or Clark. I would much prefer to learn the lessons of success and failure from the trailblazers who came before me. I study these courageous people—these geniuses and pioneers—carefully.

If I have one original idea in my lifetime, I will have made a contribution to the advancement of Western Civilization. I doubt I will ever achieve this milestone.

Einstein had an original idea: The Theory of Relativity.

But I am a person of average intelligence. I don't plan to develop any new theories in my lifetime. I will be very happy just to learn the great ideas that have already been developed—especially in the area of marketing.

For this reason, I read the great Claude Hopkins over and over again. Hopkins was perhaps the greatest advertising writer who ever lived. I also study Bob Stone and David Ogilvy. Any aspiring marketer who reads Hopkins, Ogilvy, and Stone will know most of what anyone knows about marketing today. All marketers today are still following the principles, maxims, and precepts carved out by these marketing giants. I am content to learn everything I can from these pioneers who came before me.

It took me a long time to get into Internet marketing. I spent years studying the Internet before I did much with it. I'm just starting to get into it now by carefully following the systems developed by the few who have been successful.

And guess what. The marketing principles are exactly the same as those articulated by the great ad writer Claude Hopkins at the start of the century—the last century. It's just the technology and mechanics that are different.

Chapter Four
The #1 reason mailings fail

Usually the reason for one of my mailings failing is my own ego. I was writing about what I was interested in, not what my readers were interested in. I was writing about my desires, my likes and dislikes, my goals, and my needs instead of writing about my readers' desires, goals, and needs.

The most common mistake is for the writer to write about what the writer is interested in, not what the reader is interested in. Effective sales letter writing requires that you always put yourself in the place of your reader.

You are not writing a diary. This is not creative writing. You are not writing a poem. Your job is not to amuse your reader. There's no room for self-indulgence in sales letter writing. Rhetorical flourishes and pretty prose is not rewarded here. Your one and only purpose for writing is to sell something. And there's only one way to sell: *offer something your reader needs or wants.*

How to find out what your reader needs or wants is the tricky part, which I'll cover later in this book.

How To Write...

Chapter Five
Direct mail is about basic human psychology

If you're interested in human psychology and understanding why people do the things they do, you will love direct mail marketing...because direct mail is about studying and understanding basic human psychology.

When writing my letters I must always put myself in the place of the reader. I like that about direct mail.

It forces me to go outside myself and to walk in the shoes of others. I must be an amateur psychologist to be a successful direct mail copywriter. I must understand what it is that causes people to act. I must be aware of predictable patterns of human behavior. I must get into the psyche of my reader and give my readers arguments so compelling that they will call my 1.800 number or find their checkbook, write out a check, and take the trouble to mail it to someone they don't even know, and may have never heard of.

Or, even weirder, they will go online, type their credit card information on an order form I've set up, hit a button, and send their credit card information off into cyberspace to who knows who.

Getting orders by selling through the mail is a tough task.

But it's doable, and doable on a regular basis, if you learn the laws of marketing. These laws are fixed and constant. They are the same today as they were yesterday. And they will be the same tomorrow. These laws of marketing will never change, because human nature never changes.

By this I mean that the basic dreams, aspirations, fears, and motivations of human beings will never change. They were the same in the time of Caesar. And they will be the same 100 years from now.

Technology changes over time, but basic human nature stays the same. The sales letter writer's job is to learn what it is that causes your reader to act by learning the laws of human nature, which are the iron laws of all successful marketing.

Chapter Six
Six reasons why a letter is your most powerful sales tool

1. You need very little start-up capital.

You can test market a new product or service by mailing a sales letter to a few thousand people.

If your small test mailing to your sample is successful, you can then mail to more people in your target market and be confident your mailings will continue to be successful. Of course, your rollouts and continuations must be mailed to the same "universe" (target list) of people as you mailed for your test to be valid. This is very important.

A test mailing is very much like conducting a poll of a list.

The entire science of polling is built on the principle that overall public opinion can be measured fairly accurately by asking a few hundred people what they think. Of course, the sample you are polling must be properly selected to yield a valid poll result. The same principle is the underlying foundation of all direct marketing, which banks on being able to predict future results on the basis of small test mailings into a pool of the same kinds of prospects.

I love the scientific quality of direct mail. I love what it teaches me about human nature.

Direct mail proves that human nature is fixed and constant, like the laws of gravity and physics. The entire science of direct mail is based on this truth. The laws of marketing say that human beings will respond in a certain way to certain offers, arguments, and incentives, and that people have mostly the same basic aspirations, dreams, motivations, fears, and concerns.

People behave in predictable patterns.

If your mailing to 5,000 people randomly selected from a list of 100,000 prospects works, it will work if you rollout that letter and package to the entire list.

2. You can target your market precisely.

Direct mail marketing is the opposite of broadcasting. It's "narrowcasting." Unlike television, radio, and newspaper ads—which hit everyone in a geographic region with your message—direct mail can target those most likely to buy your product. Direct mail does this by allowing you to mail specifically to those who have bought similar products in the past.

TV ads are akin to carpet-bombing. TV hits everyone, including those who have no chance of ever buying your product.

Direct mail allows you to strike your likely buyers with laser-like precision. TV ads work well for products that everyone buys, such as toothpaste, soda, hamburgers, and laundry detergent.

Direct mail works well for magazine subscriptions, newsletter subscriptions, financial services, credit card offers, specialized products, and high-end products.

For example, if you want to sell subscriptions to *Guitar* magazine, you should mail a subscription offer to people who have recently bought a guitar, not launch a major television ad campaign. The National Rifle Association looks for new members by mailing membership invitations to recent purchasers of hunting licenses and to subscribers of gun and various outdoor magazines.

The Sierra Club recruits members by sending letters to buyers of camping and hiking gear and supporters of other environmental protection groups. The AARP recruits members by sending letters and membership invitations to people who turn 55. AARP would be wasting its money by advertising on MTV.

3. Return on investment is quick, often almost immediate.

Direct mail, if done properly, is advertising that can pay for itself almost immediately.

Even with customer acquisition (also called prospect) mailings, you can sometimes break even on your cost, or even make a profit right out of the gate. But even if you return a more usual 75 cents for every one dollar spent on the standard mass-market prospecting mail program, you're doing far better than any TV, radio, or newspaper ad campaign you're likely to launch—with far less risk.

Your big return on investment then comes from repeat mailings to your customers with similar product offers. This is called your house list or housefile.

No other form of advertising brings back a better return on your investment right out of the gate.

4. It's measurable.

I know whether my direct mail package is successful based on the number of orders and replies that come in. I never have to wonder if my direct mail campaign is working. I never have to guess. Direct mail marketing is entirely measurable.

If your marketing campaign is not precisely measurable, it's really not marketing; it's public relations. I have no interest in building image or "brand awareness"—which is what traditional Madison Avenue-style advertising seeks to achieve. What I want are sales. And I want to be able to measure exactly how much I spent to bring in the order.

It's very difficult to measure the effectiveness of TV, radio, or newspaper ads. The best we can really do with these advertising media is *estimate* or *guess* how the campaign is doing.

For example, when McDonald's launches a TV ad campaign, they can't know with precision which customers are coming to their restaurants because of that particular ad campaign or which customers are coming in because of some other reason. They know they need to run ads, but they can't know exactly what their return on investment is with any particular ad campaign. So they can't precisely measure the effectiveness of their ads.

Not so with direct mail. With each mailing you know exactly what your return on investment is, because orders come back in response to a particular mailing.

Even with TV, radio, and newspaper ads that are direct-response ads, it's difficult to measure the value of customers. The problem here is how do you reach your customers again for repeat business? How do you build the equivalent of a housefile with direct response from TV, radio, or print ads?

Well, really the only way to reach your direct-response TV, radio, and newspaper ad buyers again is with mail. You have no choice but to change advertising media on your customers. You have no choice but to ask your TV responders to suddenly change their buying habits and become direct mail responders.

But the problem here is that these customers are not necessarily direct mail responsive. You know that any customer you find by mail is direct mail responsive. You don't know that with a customer you find with a TV, radio, or newspaper ad. So a customer you find with a TV, radio, or newspaper ad campaign will not be as valuable as a customer you find with a direct mail campaign.

The Internet has become a very interesting direct response marketing media, and results are measurable. But Internet marketing is very tricky, largely because people use many different email addresses and also because of anti-spamming laws and technologies.

I love the Internet as a marketing tool, but my goal is always (at least eventually) to collect actual physical postal addresses of those who respond over the Internet. An email address by itself is not very useful. I want to know exactly who and where my customers are located so I can send them postal mailings. I use the Internet mainly to support what's still the workhorse tool of the direct marketing industry. And that remains good old-fashioned direct mail.

5. Freedom and independence.

Without direct mail, your business can be held hostage by the whims of your biggest clients. If you have three clients who are buying a million dollars worth of services from you, and if this accounts for 80 percent or 90 percent of your business, you'll have no choice but to do whatever these clients or customers want you to do.

If they want you to stand on your head in the corner, you'll have to say, "For how long?" If they want you to jump around the room on one foot, wear a funny hat, and bark like a dog, you'll have to say, "Okay." Or, you'll need to find another line of work.

But if your $3 million in annual revenue comes from your list of 50,000 customers you've built with your direct mail marketing program (each of whom annually buys about $60 worth of product), you won't need to worry about any single customer pulling the plug on your business and sending you to the poor house.

And if your largest customer only represents, say, five percent of your business, you can tell the eccentric old coot to jump in the lake if he gets too nasty and demanding, and you'll feel good about it.

6. You never need to face rejection.

One of the great features of direct mail marketing is that you're never forced to face rejection. You just have to deal with those who say "yes" to your offer.

Direct mail can work if only one person out of 100 says "yes" to you and sends you a check. If you are selling a costly enough item, direct mail can work if one in 1,000 buys from you.

But if you are a salesman going door-to-door making sales pitches, it is too emotionally draining to receive one order for every 50 or 100 rejections—much less one order for every 1,000 rejections. You would become discouraged, psychologically wounded. You would likely quit before getting your first order. Arthur Miller's *Death of a Salesman* was not a happy story. But there are few experiences more exhilarating in life than the postman delivering 30 trays of mail full of "yes" answers to your letter...and checks.

Chapter Seven

The most important question you must answer before you write

You cannot write an effective sales letter until you answer one question.

Once you've answered this question, your letter will almost write itself.

This question is: **"What am I really selling?"**

Am I selling cosmetics? Or am I selling the hope of the reader becoming irresistible to men?

Am I selling clothes? Or am I selling a transformed life that will lead to romance and success?

Am I a selling a car? Or am I selling excitement, comfort, and an image for the driver?

Am I selling refrigerators? Or am I selling fewer trips to the grocery store because of all the added space, plus dramatically improving the kitchen's appearance with the fine cherry wood paneling?

Am I selling vacations? Or am I selling an experience the reader and her children will remember for the rest of their lives?

Am I selling gym memberships with treadmills and weights? Or am I selling a new body that will make male readers attractive to women and give them a longer, healthier life?

Am I selling a seminar? Or am I selling a way to give those who enroll an advantage over their peers and competitors that will last a lifetime?

Am I selling admission to Harvard? Or membership in an exclusive club that will lead to a more profitable career and open the doors of opportunity throughout life?

Am I selling a subscription to an interesting magazine? Or access to information the reader cannot do without and can't get anywhere else?

Is Starbucks selling coffee? Or is Starbucks selling an experience, a place to hang out, and even a social life?

Are florists selling roses? Or the easiest way for a guy to get back on the good side of his wife or girlfriend?

Is the phone company selling communications equipment? Or a way to stay connected to friends and loved ones?

Is Viagra selling a fix for erectile dysfunction? Or a more exciting, more enjoyable love life?

Understanding exactly what it is you are *really* selling will improve the results of your sales letters exponentially.

Chapter Eight
Your reader is not an idiot
She's your mom, your wife, your child, your friend, or your colleague

Your reader will ask two questions to qualify your letter for continued reading:

1) Is this product, service, or offer of interest to me?

2) Is this offer believable...or is it more of the usual advertising hype?

Most sales letter writers do fine with the first question. Lots of promises and hype.

Few ever really address the second question: The proof, facts, evidence, reasons.

Most sales letter writers treat their readers as though they are morons. They produce copy with fantastic claims they would be embarrassed to show their mom, their wife, their friends, their co-workers or anyone they know and respect.

When I write a letter, I have a clear picture in my mind of the person who will be reading it. For certain kinds of offers, I imagine my mom reading my letter. For other kinds of offers, I imagine my colleague receiving my letter in the mail.

Your readers are not idiots. They are very smart people who are experts at discarding hype. What they want is proof.

Raising the level of your proof and evidence is the surest way to boost your response.

Chapter Nine
"If you are selling fire extinguishers, first show the fire"

The title of this chapter is a quote from David Ogilvy, the great advertising copywriter and Madison Avenue advertising pioneer.

What Ogilvy was saying is that you should show the problem, the crisis, the threat. Then offer the solution. Don't lead by saying, "I'm selling fire extinguishers."

Lead by showing your prospects what can happen if their fire extinguishers are not in good working order, are old or worn out, or if they have the wrong fire extinguisher.

You are not selling fire extinguishers. You are selling protection for children and loved ones. You are selling protection for a home full of a lifetime of memories.

Then you can get into the merits of your fire extinguisher and into all the reasons your fire extinguisher is better than your competitor's.

Chapter Ten
The absolute necessary precondition for a sales letter to work

The greatest sales letter in the world cannot be successful without one precondition.

And that necessary precondition is this:

**For your sales letter to work, you must
enter a conversation that's already taking place in
your reader's mind.**

In other words, you must tap into a pre-existing desire.

You won't have much success selling a car to someone who is not looking to buy a car. I don't care how good your letter is.

Once you've established that this person is searching for a car to buy, the sales work can begin. You can build your case for why the car you are selling is best. But your arguments will go nowhere if your reader doesn't want a car, has a new car already, or won't be looking for a new car for several more years. Your sales pitch, no matter how skilled, is futile with this fellow.

It is also nearly impossible to sell a product that addresses a problem or need that your prospective customer has never heard of. There might be a disease out there that's getting ready to kill a million people. And you might have precisely the antidote for this disease. But if your prospect has never heard of this disease, if this disease has not been the focused attention of news coverage, then you will never be able to sell your cure.

Sales letters work because they come along at exactly the right time—a time when your reader is thinking about buying the product, or something similar, either from you or from one of your competitors. The question then is not whether your reader will buy, but *from whom* will your reader buy. If your letter comes along at just the right time; if it's convenient for your reader to buy from you; if you make a good case for your product; and if the price is right, you have a great chance to make the sale.

So to be successful, what you need is a way to find qualified leads relatively inexpensively—to find those people who want what you are selling.

I will discuss "lead generation" programs and lists in some detail later in this book—because your list is far more important than even the quality of your sales pitch.

A poor sales letter can be successful when mailed to the right list, but a great sales letter will always fail when mailed to the wrong list.

Chapter Eleven
The sales letter writer's two most important jobs

Getting and then holding a reader's attention is Job #1 for a direct mail copywriter.

Direct mail letter writing is a lot like starting a conversation in a bar with a construction worker or over a kitchen table with a mom. Your points must be clear, simple, and to the point. Sentences longer than a dozen words or so will start to lose your audience. Eyes will glaze over.

Letters must be written at a sixth grade level, or lower.

But when I say this, I am not at all suggesting that readers of my letters are stupid. Far from it. They're just busy. They don't have time to figure out what I'm trying to say. They'll give me a few seconds of their time to grab their interest.

After that, it's time to find out why water is dripping out of the ceiling, or why all those sirens are blaring across the street, or what ballgame is on the tube.

Once Job #1 is achieved, Job #2 is to present arguments and promises so compelling and so persuasive that your reader stops whatever else she's doing and sends a check to a stranger, all based on what she has read in your letter.

Chapter Twelve
Find out what your prospect wants before you write

If you don't know what your reader is looking for, you have no chance of writing a successful sales letter.

You will be throwing wild punches in the dark.

Learn what your reader wants before you write. What is his biggest fear? What is he angry about? What are his top daily frustrations? What is his #1 problem in life? What is the source of this problem?

There are many ways to do this. Are you writing to just a handful of people, or are you writing to a million people?

If you are writing to a million people, you will have to do a lot of educated guessing. You will want to write to people who have bought similar products to the one you are selling. If you are selling exercise equipment, you will want to rent lists of people who have recently bought exercise equipment.

But if you are writing to just a few people, you should talk to these people before you write. Have a conversation. Listen carefully to what they have to say. Don't interrupt. Just listen to them vent. Don't try to sell them anything. Just listen.

Listening is the most powerful sales tool there is.

Ask questions to help pinpoint their exact wants, needs, and frustrations. Then listen carefully to the answers. When your prospect answers your questions, restate back to your prospect her answers in summary form and ask her if you have correctly understood her problem.

Not only will this help you focus in like a laser on what this prospect wants, but you will be showing your prospect that you really are paying attention. This is enormously reassuring to your prospect and will encourage your prospect to keep talking—which is exactly what a great salesman wants. A great salesman is not a great talker. A great salesman is a great listener.

If you can't meet with your prospect face-to-face to have your conversation, you must find other ways to find out as much as you possibly can about the people you are writing to. What kind of business are they in? Who are their customers? What are their biggest problems likely to be?

I love to conduct surveys. This is a great way to develop "super quality" leads.

I send surveys via postal mail or email. And I call people to conduct surveys. I use banner ads on the Internet to link people to my survey. What's brilliant about a survey is that your prospect is telling you exactly what she wants. You can then tailor your letter precisely to address the wants, needs, problems, frustrations, fears, and concerns expressed by your prospects in the surveys you're conducting.

I never have much problem persuading people to participate in my surveys.

People love to give their opinions about things. They love filling out surveys if they believe the survey is real and is not just some marketing gimmick. Most people feel no one is listening to them. Many people are living lives of "quiet desperation." They welcome an opportunity to express their opinions. They welcome an opportunity to vent.

If you say you will be delivering the results of your survey to some key decision maker—perhaps Congress or the President of the United States—that's even better. Not only does your prospect get to vent, but then there's a chance your survey will have some kind of impact, actually make a difference. What you do with the results of the survey depends on the kinds of questions you're asking. But a survey where the results are going to be delivered to someone important greatly improves your chances of people filling out your poll.

It's a good idea to offer an incentive to all who participate. I usually promise to send all who participate a free copy of the final survey report. This is usually incentive enough. Plenty of people are happy to help you with your survey regardless of whether you offer an incentive. Being given the opportunity to express their opinion and to vent is often incentive enough.

What's important is for your survey to look and sound official, like a Gallup Poll. The questions must be intelligently written, focused, and on-point. They must be questions people want to answer. Your questions are very important.

The survey technique is a very powerful "lead generation" tool if used properly.

Another wonderful tool you can use is Google AdWords.

If used correctly, Google AdWords is one of the most powerful marketing tools ever devised. It's a tool that can help you develop super quality leads and even instant full-blown customers. I like it much better than the Yahoo competitor Overture, though I use both. I will explain how I use Google AdWords later in this book.

Banner ads on carefully selected Web sites (where you offer something free in exchange for your prospect filling out a survey or giving you their name and email address) can also be a very effective method of compiling your list of qualified leads. Your banner ads should appear on sites that are aligned with the product or service you are offering. This way the eyeballs that see your banner ad are likely to be connected to people who are interested in your product or service.

Writing effective Internet banner ads and designing an effective lead generation strategy through using banner ads is a science unto itself and very worthy of intense study by anyone interested in marketing. I will touch on this later in this book.

The point I want you to take away from this little section is that you must find ways to learn exactly and precisely what your prospect wants before you can write an effective sales letter, or your letter is doomed. There are all kinds of ways to do this, including:

✓ Face-to-face conversations;

✓ Surveys, polls, and questionnaires;

✓ Renting lists of people who have bought similar products and services recently;

✓ Google AdWords;

✓ Banner ads on Web sites that are related to your product;

✓ Monster.com and other job listing sites where employers are looking for people to hire to do certain jobs (Your prospects are actually telling you what they want!);

✓ The yellow pages and other category-of-business listing services, both online and offline;

✓ Classified ads;

✓ Ads in industry publications ;

✓ Referral programs (more on this later); and

✓ Searches of directories in the field of relevance.

All these are tools that can help you get inside the head of your prospect before you start writing your sales pitch. And there are many more tools you might deploy. The trick is selecting the right tool and using it effectively. If you need to drive a nail into a piece of wood, don't use a screwdriver. Use the correct tool.

To be effective in sales and marketing, you must become a detective, a private investigator. You must do a lot of legwork. You must be Sherlock Holmes. The compiling, sifting, and organizing of information on your prospects is the cornerstone of any successful marketing strategy.

If you do this correctly, your sales letters won't really need to be all that good to work pretty well. The secret to effective marketing is finding ways to get great information on your prospects, your target audience. This is where your creativity, ingenuity, and brainpower must come in.

You must use every tool available to find out who your prospects are and what they want. You must organize this information and put it in a database. And then you must use this information to help your prospects fix their problems.

Chapter Thirteen
The nine step formula for writing successful sales letters

1. Craft a great first sentence that creates intrigue.

Leading off your letter with a question is often a good device to engage the reader. Here's a pretty good one:

```
If I can show you how you can double
your income by giving me just 30 minutes
of your time a month, would you like to
learn more?
```

Questions can be effective lead sentences because you are immediately engaging your reader in a conversation. You are not preaching at your reader. You are not screaming at your reader. You are not lecturing your reader. You are asking your reader to give her opinion. You are, in effect, putting your reader in charge of the conversation. And you are doing so in a way that gets your reader thinking and imagining.

Another effective attention-getter is to start off with a damaging admission. For example:

```
If you're looking for a big prestigious
Madison Avenue ad agency to create and
conduct your ad campaign, we're not for
you.

But if you're looking for an affordable
ad agency that knows the local market
right here in Palooka, I encourage you to
check out our Web site at
AffordableAdAgency.com to pick up your
free report that will give you 10 rules
for creating great ads.
```

> Our offices are modest because we don't
> spend your hard-earned money on mahogany
> wood paneling, marble floors, fat salaries,
> and a fancy address. We use your money to
> create affordable and effective ads and
> marketing campaigns for you and your
> business.

The damaging admission is a great way to start because your honesty is disarming. By immediately revealing your weakness, your reader is far more likely to believe your claims. A damaging admission is attention-getting in itself.

Human nature is such that we all start listening intently when someone starts admitting his weaknesses, mistakes, blunders, and disasters. That's a whole lot more interesting that listening to someone prattle on about how great he is.

Or here's another way to start:

> I am writing to you because it's a matter
> of public record that you are having
> financial problems, and I think I have a way
> to help you.

This is attention-getting because you have just told your reader that you know something damaging about your reader. You have inside information about your reader. It's a bit of a shocker. Who would not keep reading after being hit on the head with such an opening line?

Yikes!

Later, I'll get more deeply into the science of crafting the opening line.

2. Figure out all the benefits of what you are selling, and promise your most important benefit first.

Notice that I use the word "benefits," not "features."

People don't buy things or products. People buy great results. You're not buying leather seats for your car; you're buying comfort, beauty, and prestige. Am I selling drivers to golfers, or am I selling long straight shots guaranteed to take balls an extra 20 yards down the fairway?

Before I start writing, I list on index cards all benefits (results) I

How To Write...

can identify the product achieving for the prospect. I then organize them in order of priority. I ask others to organize the cards in the priority they think is right. I take a kind of mini-poll—because what I think is important might very well be wrong. The larger your poll sample, the better your data will be. Ask as many people as you can to help you prioritize your benefits index cards.

If you can find a "hidden benefit," that can further strengthen your appeal. Anytime you can share a secret, show people something "hidden," ears will perk up.

A hidden benefit of aspirin is that it helps diminish the likelihood of heart attacks and strokes by thinning the blood and thereby unclogging arteries. Wow, that's a pretty good benefit. We're now supposed to take an aspirin-a-day, whether or not we have a headache. And that's great news for the aspirin makers, who were on the ropes because of Tylenol.

A hidden benefit of the time-management program you are selling is that not only will it make your reader more productive and his business more profitable, but he'll have a lot more time for family, golf, and for doing the things he loves doing.

In almost every product you sell, you can find "hidden benefits" that might be even more attractive than the obvious benefit. "Hidden benefits" are like "hidden treasures." They are so much more exciting to read about.

3. Describe your most important benefit in detail.

Your readers must be persuaded that your claims are true. You must prove your claims.

You do this by going into a fair amount of detail about how and why your product will achieve the wonderful benefit you are describing. You don't do this with a lot of hype. You don't do this by using empty words like "amazing" and "incredible." You do this with facts, reasons, and interesting little-known details.

The great advertising writer Claude Hopkins, way back in 1919, was hired by Schlitz beer to craft an ad campaign that would rescue the company. Schlitz at the time was running about fifteenth in beer sales and was in deep trouble.

Hopkins made a trip to Wisconsin to visit the brewery. He needed to learn more about how beer was made. Hopkins knew that it was impossible to sell without a thorough knowledge of the product being sold.

The folks at Schlitz showed Hopkins the entire brewing process, step by step. They showed him how deep they had drilled their wells to find the purest water. They showed him the glass enclosed rooms that kept the water pure, the kind of yeast they used and where they got it. They showed Hopkins the place where the bottles were cleaned, re-cleaned, and sanitized a dozen times.

"My God," Hopkins said, "Why don't you tell people in your advertising about all these steps you are taking to brew your beer?"

But, answered the Schlitz people, "all companies brew their beer about the same way."

"Yes," Hopkins countered, "but the first one to tell the public about this process will gain a big advantage."

Hopkins then launched an ad campaign for Schlitz that described in detail the company's step-by-step brewing process for making the beer. Within six months, Schlitz jumped to the #1 selling beer.

Hopkins proved with his ad campaign that there are no boring subjects, just boring writers.

"Who wants to hear a story about the step-by-step brewing process of making beer?" one might wonder.

Turns out those who love beer are fascinated by the subject.

They want to know exactly and precisely why they should pick this beer above all others. Claude Hopkins understood this law of marketing and went on to turn the brewing process into an exciting story, full of detail—and of riveting interest to beer lovers.

4. Tell readers exactly what they will get.

Your customers want to know exactly what they will be getting for their money.

When you buy a car, you want the exact specifications, so that when you compare prices with other dealers you know you are comparing apples to apples. When you buy a computer, you need to know the specifications: How fast is it? How much memory does it have? How big is the screen? How clear is the resolution?

Include all the information. If the information is highly technical, such as with computers, you should include this on a separate insert, perhaps along with a beautiful and impressive photo of the computer you are selling. Technical specifications make for boring copy, so the complete list should not be included in the letter, just the highlights. But a complete list should be included somewhere.

If you are selling a seminar on tape or a study-at-home course, you should include an impressive photo of all the materials that will be arriving in a box. Your letter, your sales package, is like a show-and-tell presentation. Provide all the information—if not all in the letter, on separate inserts and enclosures. Give your reader a lot of great material to study.

5. Provide third-party testimony to the truth of your claims.

Anything the salesman has to say is going to be met with skepticism, no matter how compelling the story and claims, and no matter how exact the details are described.

You need others—preferably famous and respected people—to confirm that what you are saying is true.

If you are selling a fix for muscle pain, you should have endorsements by top doctors—perhaps doctors who work for professional sports teams. An endorsement of your muscle pain cure from the official team doctor of the New York Giants would be impressive.

But it's also important for endorsements not to be just hype. Endorsements are best if they are mini-stories—a mini-story on how the recognized expert discovered your product and then a fairly detailed description of exactly what your product achieved for him is an effective, believable testimonial.

The more testimonials you have the better. I sometimes include an entire booklet of testimonials with my mailings. I feel I can never have enough testimonials. I also try to secure testimonials on audio and video and put them on my Web site. Sometimes I'll include a CD, DVD, or VHS videotape with my mailing that includes all my testimonials, accompanied by the printed version (because I know most people will not take the time to view the DVD).

6. Tell readers what bad things will happen if they fail to act now.

Your readers must be given good reasons to act now, not tomorrow. People buy more out of impulse. If your prospect puts your letter aside, thinking she will get to it later, your offer is probably doomed. Your reasons to act now, not tomorrow, must also be credible, not hype. For example:

> The registration deadline for my Direct Marketer's Boot Camp is September 23. I'm limiting enrollment to just 24 people to ensure that each participant receives personal one-on-one coaching, which includes an analysis of your current direct marketing offers.
>
> I am accepting enrollment applications in the order of their arrival. The Boot Camps always fill up long before the deadline date. So I encourage you to send me your application as soon as you possibly can. You should do so today. To enroll immediately, you can also call me at 1.800._____ or enroll online at: **www.website.com.**

Can you see how the reason I give for my reader to answer my letter immediately also restates some of the key benefits of the seminar? In this case, it is the personal one-on-one coaching and analysis of the customer's current direct marketing offers. I might also mention that "this is the last time I've scheduled a Boot Camp in the Cleveland area. I'm sure I'll be back again, but maybe not for another couple of years."

Suggesting to your reader that this is a "last chance" opportunity to do something or buy something is always strong. When *Seinfeld*, or *M*A*S*H*, or *Dallas* announced their last and final shows, when we were told there would never be another show made, these last and final programs were some of the most widely-watched TV shows in history.

You might not be looking to buy a gun. You might never have thought of buying a gun before. But what if you knew that all gun purchases would be banned after tomorrow? And that after tomorrow, you would never be allowed to buy another gun? You would see a stampede into gun stores.

"Last chance" arguments for acting now is a proven formula for success. But, as with all your sales letters and presentations, the claim must be believable.

Avoid using shopworn phrases used by amateur writers like "Supplies are limited, so act now." Everyone knows you probably have a warehouse full of the junk. Stronger would be a more credible,

```
    We're down to the last few books, and it
    could be many months before we go back up
    on press with another printing.

    So I encourage you to get your order in
    today. Calling us as at 1.800.____ or
    ordering online at www.website.com is the
    surest and fastest way to secure your book.
```

This says almost same thing, but it's far more precise. The reasons are solid. And there's no hype, just good solid facts and reasons for acting now and not waiting until tomorrow.

7. Rephrase the most prominent benefits in the close and in other parts of the package.

Repeating your message is crucial in all successful marketing. But don't repeat the same words all the time or you will bore your reader. Look for new, fresh ways to underscore what your offer is and what the benefits are. This is where brainpower and creativity come in.

You do this in your lead. You back up your claims in the body of your letter, in the enclosures and testimonials. And you summarize your offer, restating the principal benefit in the P.S. and on the order form.

What you are offering, what you are selling, must be crystal clear in about three seconds. Your reader must never need to search for what you are selling.

8. Include a money-back guarantee.

This is absolutely essential, because you are asking your reader, who may never have met you, to trust your claims and send you money. And, as with everything else in your letter, you must make your guarantee believable. Your reader must feel absolutely certain that this guarantee you are describing is real. It must be unconditional, no questions asked.

The guarantee should be a stand-alone certificate, signed by the letter signer. It should be on nice paper and look something like a stock certificate or a U.S. savings bond. It should look like an official document from the U.S. Treasury. It should look like it has real monetary value just by itself. It should look something like money. This will grab the attention of your reader and reassure your reader.

You might take your guarantee and assurance of satisfaction one step further. "If you are ever having any problems with this product, please call me directly. The direct line to my desk is _____. If you don't reach me there, my cell phone number is _____."

And you might make this promise: "If you are unhappy in any way with my service, just write 'cancel' on my invoice and mail it back to me. You'll owe nothing for the month."

Or: "If you ever have a problem that we cannot fix within 24 hours, I'll give you that month's service for free. And you will continue to receive free service until we fix the problem to your satisfaction."

Always put the buyer in charge of the guarantee and the decision as to whether a refund is called for.

9. Offer instant gratification.

In the 21st Century, the age of high-speed Internet and overnight delivery, you must offer instant gratification. People today are not patient. They are not willing to "allow four-to-six weeks for delivery." That's like waiting until the next life.

Always be sure to include a toll-free phone number and Web site order form so they can order immediately. And offer an overnight delivery option. People want their TV programs now, today, not several days from now when the cable hook-up guy can get to it.

So when your sales letter is mailed, be sure you are ready to fulfill orders instantly.

Chapter Fourteen
Seventeen reasons people buy

1. Fear

People buy because they fear getting old, fear going broke, fear being left behind. They fear being left out. They fear death. They fear getting sick, fear going to Hell, fear being alone. They fear Republicans gaining power, or they fear Democrats gaining power.

They fear the Nazis or Communists gaining power. They fear life is meaningless. They fear failure. They fear their kids won't amount to anything. They fear being insignificant, not leaving a mark. Fear comes in all shapes, sizes, and forms. Fear is a powerful motive causing people to buy.

2. Desire to be recognized

People buy because they want honor and prestige. They want recognition. They want to be set apart from the crowd. They want to be part of an exclusive, prestigious club. They want fame.

3. Greed

Just about everyone wants more money. No matter how rich someone is, they always want more. Even billionaires want more, not because they need it, just because they want it. They want more than the other billionaire has. Warren Buffet has not stopped trying to make more money even though he's the second richest man in the world. Bill Gates still wants more because he wants to stay the richest.

Ten thousand pairs of shoes were not enough for Imelda Marcos. She always wanted more shoes.

4. Love

Love is a powerful motivator to buy. What other motive can there be for buying life insurance? People want to make sure their children have the best and that their loved ones are taken care of.

5. Self-improvement

People always want to improve themselves. They join a gym to get in shape. They sign up for a seminar to learn something that will help them get ahead. "How To" manuals are some of the best selling books on Amazon.

6. Desire to win

There's a strong competitive instinct in most people. People just flat out want to win at games, sports, business, love, and in life. No one wants to be called a "Loser."

People want to be the best. They want the recognition that goes with winning, or they just want the satisfaction of knowing they are the best at something. It's not enough for Tiger Woods to be the best golfer in the world. He now wants to be the best golfer of all time. Does he want to win because he wants more fame or more money? Does winning make him feel superior to other people? I don't think so. I think he is someone who sets a goal and then just wants to achieve it. He's a perfectionist. He feels he can always do better.

The desire to win will cause people to buy the best equipment, get the best teacher, buy the best books and videos on the subject. We want our kids to win. We want our teams to win. The innate desire most of us have to win fuels the sports industry and much of our economy.

7. Comfort

People want comfort. They want a comfortable bed, a comfortable chair, a comfortable car, comfortable shoes, comfortable clothes. People want a Jacuzzi. We want pain relievers even for the most minor pains, just to make ourselves more comfortable. We want larger and more comfortable rooms. Americans, especially, seem to be on a never-ending quest for more and more comfort.

8. Laziness

Sure people want to improve themselves, and they want to win, and they want to make more money...but only if it's easy.

People are lazy. That's why you don't see many sales pitches that highlight how hard you must work to achieve the results promised. You will see beautiful people sitting on the exercise equipment and talking more often than we see them actually using it. People want the results without the work. "Lose 10 pounds in 30 days with no dieting or exercise. Just take this pill." That's the basic pitch.

9. Quest for a great experience

People want great experiences they will remember for the rest of their lives. They want travel experiences, educational experiences, family outings, parties, vacations, barbecues, great food at great restaurants, and good movies to watch.

They want exciting experiences, relaxing experiences, social experiences, and entertainment experiences. People want shared experiences with loved ones. The travel and entertainment industry is all about creating and selling memorable experiences.

10. Sex

People want more sex and better sex. People want sex, period. People want to be more attractive and sexier. Sex is everywhere in advertising, movies, and entertainment. Sometimes it's out in the open, sometimes implied. The mere mention of the word "sex" draws immediate and riveted attention.

11. The desire for relationships

People want friends. People want dates. People want romance. People want to get married. People want to be connected to other people. People want to be part of a community. Dating sites are among the most popular on the Internet. People want to improve their relationships with their children and with their spouse. When a relationship breaks up, it's very painful. When a relationship starts, it's exciting. Most people do not want to be alone in the world.

12. Anger

Anger can be a very strong motivator. People send money to the Republican Party because they are angry at the Democrats. People send money to the Democratic Party because they are angry at the Republicans. People hire a lawyer to sue someone because they are angry. Following the 9/11 terrorist attack on America, people bought flags and decals not just out of patriotism, but also to show their anger at the terrorists. That was certainly righteous anger. Anger makes people want to strike back and fight, even go to war.

13. Desire to make a difference

People want their lives to count for something, to make a difference.

People run for President and public office to make a difference, hopefully not just for recognition. People contribute to charities, political causes, and religious organizations to make a difference. People become teachers and religious leaders to make a difference. People write books and articles to make a difference. People volunteer to make a difference.

Very few people want their life to count for absolutely nothing, to have made no positive impact in the world. Most people want to leave a legacy of some kind.

The desire to have an impact, to leave a mark, to make the world a better place can be a powerful motivator to buy or contribute.

14. Desire for meaning in life

People want life to mean something.

Religious organizations rely on this motive to prosper. Most people believe in God. Most people do not want to believe their life is an accident. People buy Bibles, religious tracts, and philosophical discourses to find meaning in life. They join a church and attend seminars for the same reason.

Billions of dollars are spent every year by people wanting to find meaning in life.

15. Desire for power

People want to tell others what to do. They want to be in charge. They want power. They want to be like God. Sometimes they want power to do good things, sometimes evil things.

Elections are about deciding who will be in charge. Billions of dollars are spent to win elections, win power. People start their own businesses and organizations in part because they want to be the boss. People want to be in charge of their own lives, and in charge of other people's lives as well.

Serial killers are the way they are because they want power over others, their victims. The desire for power over others is at the root of every war. The obsession for power has caused enormous human misery: Hitler, Stalin, Mao Tse Tung, Pol Pot and countless dictators throughout history. Thank heavens, in America we have found a way to prevent anyone from getting too much power.

The desire for power is one of the most powerful human motives.

16. Necessity of life

People need food, water, soap, clothes, electricity, gas, transportation, haircuts, and phones. Maybe computers and Internet connections now fall under the category of a necessity of modern life. Businesses need paper, copiers, desks, chairs, fax machines, phones, and computers.

"Can't do without it" is certainly a powerful reason to buy.

17. Addiction

People become addicted to drugs, alcohol, tobacco, caffeine, gambling, pornography, sex, and fast food. Some addictions are physical, others psychological. But the effect is the same, an ever-present compulsion to get more.

Marketers of these products see their job as feeding the addiction and creating more addicts to the substance, product, or activity. This is how the drug dealers, the tobacco and alcohol companies, the porn industry, sex traffickers, the casinos, and the fast food and junk food companies are raking in billions of dollars.

Chapter Fifteen
The #1 reason people buy

In the previous section I list 17 motives fueling the desire of people to buy something. But almost all of these can be recast and placed under one motive.

The most powerful motive of all is **fear**.

People are very insecure about their place in life.

Are people searching for love, or are they more afraid of ending up alone?

Stopping something bad from happening is always a more powerful motivator than causing something good to happen. I exercise not so I can look like Mr. Universe, but because I fear looking like Jabba the Hut. I want to make more money not so I can buy more things, but mostly to guard against going broke.

I use Rogaine because I fear losing all my hair. I've lost most of my hair anyway, and I don't think the stuff works. But I fear what might happen if I stop using it, so I keep buying the junk. I think I'll just shave my head and rid myself of that concern once and for all.

Desire for power is a subset of fear. So is anger. People are angry because they are not in control. Short people (i.e. Hitler, Stalin, Napoleon, Mao Tse Tung, Pol Pot) seem more interested in power than tall people (Thomas Jefferson, George Washington). People want power and get angry mostly because they are insecure—which is a variation of the fear motive.

Your sales letters will perform far better if you talk about, or imply, all the bad things that will happen to your reader if he fails to answer your letter. If you receive a letter from the IRS or an attorney, you are very likely to open it—far more likely than a letter from Bloomingdales.

People fear the IRS, fear lawsuits, fear getting older, fear dying, fear failing, fear loneliness, fear nature, fear getting sick, fear God, fear going to Hell, fear being left behind or left out, and fear being fired. They fear not keeping up with the Joneses, fear not amounting to anything in life, fear for their kids, fear not being understood, fear other people, fear walking down the street, and just generally fear life. Woody Allen built a career on making movies about people's fears, insecurities, and neuroses.

The news media sells almost nothing but fear, because news organizations know that fear sells.

Rarely do we hear a positive news story. Mostly we hear stories about disasters, crimes, wars, typhoons, disease. People contribute to causes mostly because they want to stop something bad from happening.

How does the car salesman stop you from walking out of the showroom?

> "Another guy also loved this car and says he'll be back later today with his down payment. If you don't buy it now, this car will be gone this evening."

Or...

> "This deal I'm offering you expires at the end of the month, which is today. We're actually losing money on this price. We're only offering this price today so we can meet our sales quota for the month because if we meet our quota, we get a bonus from GM."

I'm sure you've heard these or similar pitches before.

The salesman is using fear (your fear of losing out) as a way to persuade you to make an immediate decision.

People buy not so much to gain something, but because they fear losing something important if they don't buy.

Chapter Sixteen
How to construct your offer

A great offer can succeed with poor copy.

But the best copy in the world cannot sell a poor offer.

This is another way of saying, "people are not idiots." They count their pennies. They make mathematical calculations before parting with their hard-earned money. They want the best deal. If they find a better deal somewhere else, they'll take it.

The challenge is constructing an irresistible offer that won't bankrupt you. If I said, "Here, have a free Ferrari," you would certainly take it and not believe your good fortune. But that would not make much business sense for me.

Price

Price is a critical consideration in constructing your offer. Your price must be high enough so as to allow sufficient mark-up, while not so high as to discourage buyers. What is your ideal price to charge? Industry standard is one way to measure. I always prefer testing—trial and error.

Shipping and handling

Do you include it in the price of your product? Or do you pad some profit in your shipping and handling charge? Shipping and handling is a significant cost.

Unit of sale

Are you selling one at a time? A "two for the price of one" deal? Do you offer a bulk rate discount? This will depend on the product you are selling and test results. You might want to keep your offer simple and just offer one unit. You might confuse your reader by offering too many options.

Offering choices often depresses sales. Plus, selling one unit at a time might allow you to capture more customers, which might be more important than moving a lot of this particular product. So decide what your primary goal is and drive toward that target. Don't try to achieve more than one objective with your sales letter.

Options and extras

It's usually best to highlight only the basic price of the product in your advertising, and then sell additional options and extras after the customer has made a decision to buy the basic product. You'll never see an ad for a car with the price of the car as it would be fully loaded. The price advertised is usually the lowest it can possibly be without any "extras." The extras are sold at the point of sale. "Would you like leather seats? How about cruise control and electric windows?" All this is extra and adds to the basic price.

The up-sell

This is a little different from the options and extras listed above. With this approach you reel in your customer with your lower priced product and, on the phone or in person, attempt to sell him a more expensive product or an additional related product. You're in the golf store buying a sand wedge. The salesman says, "Would you like to try this incredible driver?" You're at McDonald's buying a quarter-pounder. "Would you also like some fries? How about a drink? Have you tried our new Oreo cookie shake?"

Over time, you will learn what percentage of customers you can up-sell. This will increase the value of your average customer. And this will change your calculations as to how much you can spend to acquire a customer. The up-sell potential can affect how you calculate and frame your initial offer.

Future obligation

"Choose any of these four best-selling books and pay just 10 cents, and agree to buy four more over the next 12 months."

This offer is common for book clubs and tape/CD/DVD clubs. These offers require the seller to take a short-term loss in exchange for a long-term payoff.

Pay over time

If you are selling an expensive item, offering the option of paying in monthly installments is often a good idea. Consumers have become used to automatic monthly charges being billed to their credit card. $395 for an item is a hefty check for a consumer to write all at once. But $32.91 charged each month for 12 months to a credit or debit card sounds like about what I might be paying for my gym membership or cable TV bill. It's a lot more palatable and won't stand out on my monthly credit card billing statement.

The "Bill Me Later" option is often used for subscription offers. Sellers of big-ticket durable items, such as furniture and washing machines, will sometimes hype "No payments for a year."

Most of us would much rather pay later than pay now; and pay monthly rather than pay all at once.

Free trial

Try this:

```
Your three-month trial subscription is
free. If you decide National Review
magazine is not for you, just write
'cancel' on the 12-month subscription
invoice we'll be sending you in 90 days
after your three-month trial subscription
has run out.
```

No fee, 0% interest rate

No annual fee is typical of credit card offers. If you read the fine print, what you will find is the "no annual fee" offer is usually replaced by a higher interest rate. Or if there's a 0% interest rate offered, it's an introductory interest rate and will soon go up to ordinary levels, or possibly extraordinary levels.

You'll sometimes see 0% financing for offers by auto dealers. This is an eye-catcher, but just understand that the cost of offering a 0% interest rate must be captured somewhere else: higher price for the car, bigger down payment requirement. But these can be effective offers, mostly because they are eye-catching.

Pre-approved

This is another staple of credit card marketing. What the marketer is telling us is that there will be no hard work involved in getting this card—no pain-in-the neck application to fill out. Just tell us you want the card and we'll send it to you.

This approach is also taken by retailers who offer special store credit cards that are good only in that store.

Mail-in rebate

The mail-in cash rebate offer allows the marketer to hype a lower price, a tactic that is often used by sellers of computers, software, televisions, and electronics equipment. The ad will hype the price of the computer as "**$850** after your $100 mail-in cash rebate."

Notice the tiny print.

So you still have to pay $950 for the computer, and then jump over all kinds of hurdles and wait for weeks or even months for your $100 to be refunded. Many of these companies make it so difficult to get the cash rebate that buyers just give up. You have to mail in your receipt (the original, not a copy), cut the bar code off the carton, find the serial number of the product, write the name and address of the store where you bought the product, list the name of the salesman, and then wait eight weeks. You will then likely get a notice telling you no rebate is coming because you missed some step. You then have no chance of fixing the problem because you've already sent them your original receipt and bar code from the carton.

I'm not a fan of the rebate tactic because most often it's a lie. The price hyped in the ad is really not the price.

Free gift

Enclosing a free gift with your sales letter is a good way to draw attention to your letter and to illustrate what you are selling.

If you're in the office product supply business, sending your customers and prospects a pocket calendar or a pen with the name, address, and phone number of the store printed on it can work well. Giving away coffee mugs that advertise your business can also be a nice touch. And there's a chance your coffee mug, with your business's name prominently displayed, will stay on your prospect's desk all year, or at least be stored with all his other coffee mugs and seen on occasion.

I have enclosed nice coffee mugs and cups with my sales appeals to great effect. The free gift gets attention for my letter, and the coffee cup, especially if it's one of those nice thermal ones that keeps your coffee warm and fits well into a coffee cup holder in a car, is appreciated.

If you develop an especially nice and useful free gift, this can actually become part of your brand. One fellow I know who runs a non-profit organization is a beekeeper as a hobby. He sends a jar of honey from his beehives every year to his best donors. This is the kind of thoughtful free gift everyone who receives it remembers and appreciates. It sure works well for him.

Perhaps the best use of the free gift is the free toy McDonald's gives away with its Happy Meals. The little kids are more interested in getting the toy than the meal. What McDonald's is doing is hooking kids on fast food at an early age with the toy. The kids then drag their parents to McDonald's so the kids can get the toy. It's a brilliant marketing strategy, using the kids to get parents to bring the entire family to McDonald's, that then become lifelong memories—family traditions. It's also why Americans are getting so fat, but that's a topic outside the scope of this book.

The free prize in Cracker Jack is another example, as is the comic in Bazooka Joe bubble gum, and the secret decoder ring hidden in the kids' cereal box. Skillful use of the free gift for the right products can significantly boost your response. People just love gifts and prizes.

Free extras

If you are selling a subscription to a newsletter or magazine, your offer will almost always do better if you add several free extras, such as a free special report and free book. These free extras should be precisely on point with the main product you are selling. Don't throw in a free toaster with your newsletter subscription offer.

Infomercials will always toss in plenty of free extras, often as incentives for responding immediately. Sometimes the free extras sound more appealing than the main product. In addition to this miracle knife, "you will get this set of six beautiful steak knives absolutely free if you call this number today, plus you will receive...You will also receive...And here's another thing you will get..." The impression the offer leaves is that you will be showered with a lot of valuable free stuff if you call right now.

Incentives

Banks and credit card companies want you to use their credit card, and not someone else's. So they offer incentives. You might get frequent flier miles—attractive if you fly a lot.

So this is an offer made mostly to affluent people who travel often, either on business or for vacation. Discover offers "cash back" for using its card. This probably appeals more to lower income folks who place greater value on having a few extra bucks in their pocket. American Express lets you select items from a product catalogue if you rack up enough "rewards points."

I don't like this offer much. I never have time to go through the catalogue and it seems you have to rack up an awful lot of points to qualify for anything worthwhile. I like frequent flier miles. This incentive, however, is putting the beleaguered airline industry under financial pressure, so they keep putting more and more restrictions on how frequent flier miles can be used.

Sweepstakes

Reader's Digest builds its subscription list almost entirely with a sweepstakes offer. Publisher's Clearing House offers subscriptions to many different magazines with its sweepstakes contest. With the sweepstakes appeal, the main event is the sweepstakes contest, while the subscription offer is the sideshow.

Sweepstakes offers work best for low-priced items. And the items must be useful to everyone. *Reader's Digest* is the kind of magazine that anyone would enjoy. A sweepstakes offer would not work as well for selling a specialty publication.

Sweepstakes appeals only work well when mailed to lists built by other sweepstakes offers. There is a segment of the population that is fanatical about playing sweepstakes contests. They will play just about every sweepstakes contest they can get their hands on.

And if the product seems worthwhile, they will throw a few bucks into the reply envelope to buy it. It's an impulse purchase—like picking up a packet of Gummy Bears while going through the checkout line at the supermarket. You don't go into the store expecting to buy the Gummy Bears, but you saw them sitting there, so grabbed a packet. That's basically how the sweepstakes contest works.

There is also a nagging suspicion in the back of the mind of the sweepstakes player that buying the product, whatever it is, might improve the odds of winning. Even though the letter and the copy throughout the sweepstakes package is very clear that buying will not improve the odds of winning, that all responders have an equal chance of winning whether they buy or not, some sweeps players still believe buying the product will improve their chance of winning. And if the product looks useful anyway, there's no harm in buying it if it only costs a few bucks.

Sweepstakes offers have become increasingly popular on the Internet as an incentive for people to supply their email address, and perhaps also to fill out a survey. What the sweepstakes sponsor is doing is collecting valuable marketing information on the sweeps players so they can come back at them later with more precisely targeted sales pitches.

Money-back guarantee

I mentioned the money-back guarantee in the previous section as one of the essential elements of sales letters offering products through the mail. But it's also part of the offer—that is, part of your business calculation. Some will ask for their money back. You'll need to factor this into your business plan. If you are selling to consumers through the mail or online, you won't succeed without a money-back guarantee. Everyone expects it. It's a cost of doing business.

* * * *

The writing and creative work cannot begin until you have decided the offer. How much can you spend to acquire a customer? How good a deal can you really afford to give? What is the likely long-term value of the average new customer to you?

These are critical questions you must answer when constructing your offer. And you must continuously test offers and various combinations of offers.

Also, keep this in mind:

Whatever method you use to bring your customers in the door is how you will need to sell to them in the future. If you brought them in with free gifts, you will need to keep giving them free gifts. Children will be devastated if McDonald's stops giving out toys. The toy is now part of the McDonald's experience. If you brought your customers in with sweepstakes offers, you'll need to keep giving them sweepstakes contests to play. If they came in with "pay over time" or "installment" pay offers, that's what you will need to give them from here on out—forever.

So whatever offer, or combination of offers, you select to bring in your customers, you must stick with it.

Chapter Seventeen

Positioning

"Positioning" is the most critical issue** to settle before you begin your marketing and before you construct offers to test.

And the reason is this:

An offer is not just about price and terms.

Sometimes if you charge too little, people value your service less. If your surgeon only charges you $25 per hour for his work, you might appreciate his low price, but you would certainly decline his service. "How can he charge so little if he's any good?" you would think.

On the other hand, if he's charging you $500 per hour, you might gasp at the price, but accept it, knowing his price is high because he's the very best at what he does, and you certainly want the very best surgeon operating on you.

Are Gucci shoes and handbags really worth the staggering price? Are Gucci products really that much better than other brands that are a third the price? Gucci's products look pretty flimsy to me. Gucci's entire marketing appeal is that its products are ridiculously over-priced. Apparently, that's part of what people want when they buy Gucci. The Gucci label shouts to their friends: "Look at me. See how much I paid for this. I must have so much money I don't know what to do with it all."

I don't understand this desire people have to advertise to everyone that they've spent too much on a handbag. "I've just been ripped off" is what these people are telling me. "I'm a complete idiot," is the message I'm getting from them. But there it is—Gucci's entire marketing pitch in a nutshell.

Diamonds are not really rare stones at all. But DeBeers has figured out how to create a near monopoly on the production and supply of diamonds. Then DeBeers figured out how to market diamonds not just as rare, but as a way for men to show their love for a woman. "A diamond is forever." Actually, diamonds are common.

So the question of price is not necessarily always about how low the price is compared to your competitors, but about the "positioning" of your product in people's minds. The question of how you "position" your product or service is the most important issue you must settle before you begin your marketing efforts.

Gucci is not really selling shoes and handbags. Gucci is selling image. DeBeers is not really selling clear, sparkling stones. DeBeers is selling "proof that he loves me."

Chapter Eighteen
Figure out your unique selling proposition (USP)

What is it that's different about your business, your product, your service?

What is it that your product does that no other product does?

What makes you different from your competitors?

We marketers toss around the term "unique selling proposition" all the time. But I've found very few small businesses that can tell me in 50 words or less why I (or any other consumer) should buy from them as opposed to all the other choices I have.

All this takes is a little thought and creativity.

Maybe what makes you different is that you are local. Or maybe you're different because you're national. Maybe your advantage is that you're small, or that you're big. Maybe your advantage is that your staff is old and "experienced" or that your staff is young and "energetic."

If I were to start a competitor to the National Rifle Association, I would not start an organization that does exactly what the NRA does. I would try to figure out what needs to be done in the Second Amendment arena that the NRA isn't doing. I would try to find a task that needs doing that no one else is working on.

Perhaps I would try to be even more hardcore and purest on the Second Amendment issue than the NRA. By taking this approach, I would never become as big as the NRA, but I might become 20 percent or 10 percent the size of the NRA.

I would try to find some niche to dominate and become known for, some niche not occupied by the NRA. It would be hopeless to try to compete directly with the NRA, as hopeless as it would be to try to compete with Coca-Cola by launching an imitation cola.

Yes, other companies have done it. Pepsi did it successfully with many billions of dollars in advertising. Of course, Pepsi will never surpass Coke. Pepsi will always be the #2 cola drink, and that's not bad. But even Pepsi emphasizes its differences with Coke. Pepsi is "less syrupy," has a "cleaner, more refreshing taste," "is chosen by 70 percent of people in blind taste tests," and is for a "younger generation" —or so the company claims.

Pepsi never says it is the same as Coke, but rather claims to taste better than Coke.

But most of us don't have billions of dollars to compete with the Coca-Colas of the world, so we need to do something different, something that's clearly not being done by some other organization that's a lot bigger and richer than we are.

So figure out, or manufacture, what makes you different from your competition, and hammer your theme into the minds of your customers and potential customers with relentless repetition. Of course, your USP must be a difference that's both needed and sellable. No point in having a USP no one wants, like diet pizza. But that's another discussion.

Chapter Nineteen
Sell just one thing

Never try to sell two things in a direct mail package.

The mind can grasp one thing at most. You would never want to say, "From me, you can buy a BMW or toothpaste."

Sell one product, one service. And be as specific as possible. Specialists make more money than generalists. Neurosurgeons make more money than general practitioners. The more narrow your focus, the more successful you will be. People want a plumber to fix their plumbing problem, not a jack-of-all-trades handyman.

Narrow is the gate to paradise. Focus your message like a laser. And keep it simple. This rule is Direct Marketing 101.

By the way, catalogues are not an exception to this rule.

Catalogues, of course, sell more than one thing. They sell many different items. But successful catalogues are really selling one overarching idea or theme. Successful catalogues sell one image, one theme, one concept. And all the products should fit into that theme, or

USP.

So, in the final analysis, even catalogues must sell a single, narrow theme to be successful, and not try to be all things to all people (for example, Sharper Image, LL Bean, Lands' End). The more a catalogue company diverts from its single easy-to-understand theme and tries to become all things to all people, the quicker it will fail—for example, Sears.

Chapter Twenty
Give away your ideas and products

Don't be afraid to give away your products and ideas for free.

If what you are selling is good, especially if it's really great, give your ideas and products away. Your customers won't be able to get enough.

How do drug dealers create drug addicts? They give the stuff away, for a while. If a company launches a new brand of coffee, they give it away, for a while. If you were to launch a new sport that no one had heard of, you would let people experience it for free, for a while.

Your sales letters, in essence, are proposals, show-and-tell presentations. So you will need to give away some valuable information. Sure, some of your prospects will steal your ideas and not pay you for them. That's just the cost of doing business. There are some people out there who want whatever they can get for free—the "something for nothing crowd." But you will also find gold out there, those who will appreciate you for your work and what you can do, and who will be more than happy to pay you for what you are selling.

My #1 rule for success in business is: "Don't focus on your own problems and your own needs, but focus instead on helping others fix their problems." If you do that well, your problems will be fixed along the way. So don't worry that some of your prospects will just rip-off your ideas and not pay you for them.

My response to that is not to yell, scream, and cry, but simply to say, "Glad I helped." And isn't it best if you find out early what people are like, rather than find out later when they might owe you a lot of money?

Chapter Twenty-One
When you build a relationship, you have no competition

The goal of all your marketing should be to build relationships not just make sales. Relationships are much more valuable than sales. A sale is a one-time occurrence, but a relationship can last a lifetime.

People would much rather do business with those they know.

With this principle in mind, you should not view your sales letter as a one-time event, but as the start of a conversation. You are trying to start a dialogue with your prospect, a dialogue that will develop into a long-term relationship.

Chapter Twenty-Two
Write as people actually speak in everyday life

In your sales letters, use regular conversational language.

Don't write as your high school English teacher or your college English professor would want you to write.

Write as people actually speak when having a conversation on a street corner. I write my letters as I would write to my mom or a close friend. I now write at a sixth grade level, not because people are unintelligent, but because people simply don't have the time or patience to figure out what I am trying to say. They don't have time to unscramble the King's English.

Your mission is not to impress your reader with your intelligence. Your mission as a writer of sales letters is to communicate your message as simply and directly as possible.

Always maintain the personal tone of your letter. Instead of saying "we" or "us," use the word "I." Letters should be one-on-one communications.

The phrase "you and I" can be found throughout my sales letters. It can sound redundant at times, but the "you" and "I" words are essential for making letters sound personal.

I think the best writers of sales letters are people with blue-collar backgrounds who are used to talking with longshoremen, construction workers, and people at sports bars (where I like to hang out). The best direct mail copywriters are not people with Ivy League educations, or even any college education. A salesman who sells vacuum cleaners door to door and is used to talking with housewives everyday about his product would likely make an excellent writer of sales letters.

A writer of great sales letters need not be able to deliver an esoteric lecture to a room full of college professors. In fact, anyone who can do that should probably select a field other than direct mail copywriting. A direct mail copywriter must know how to have a casual conversation with average, everyday folks who have everyday concerns and problems.

Chapter Twenty-Three
Write a package, not just a letter

The letter is the heart of your package. The letter is certainly the most important element of your package. But your package contains other key components, including an order form or reply form and a carrier envelope at a bare minimum.

I almost always include a variety of inserts, perhaps photographs, testimonials, a certificate highlighting the money-back guarantee, perhaps some kind of lift note, a manila folder full of press clippings on the product, a FAQ booklet, maybe even a CD, DVD, or VHS video tape.

Your direct mail marketing piece is a show-and-tell presentation.

No matter what element of the package the reader picks up, the reader should be hit over the head with the same message. Never have different messages and different themes conveyed with your inserts. With every direct mail offer, you must market one and only one concept, one Big Idea. Keep your message simple and focused. The purpose of every element of the package is to underscore the one single overarching reason you are writing.

Some inserts can reinforce different aspects of the one Big Idea you are selling. For example, testimonials and track records show the reader that your product has a history of achieving all the great things you are claiming. But testimonials and track records must be directly on point with the theme of your letter. If the focus of your organization is finding a cure for cancer, don't insert a track record on your success with assisting hospitalized veterans.

Any insert or enclosure that is off-point, even slightly, will distract and confuse your readers, can undermine your credibility, and will depress returns.

Chapter Twenty-Four
Generate emotion

People buy more from impulse than from careful analysis of facts. They buy it because they want it. Sure, you need facts, arguments, reasons, and logic. But these things alone will leave the reader feeling cold.

Most great salesmen not only know their product thoroughly, they are excited about their product. They have stories to tell about folks who have bought the product and the great things the product has done for them. Great salesmen are likeable, believable people who are comfortable talking with longshoremen, housewives, doctors, or college professors. Great salesmen are happy, optimistic people. Their enthusiasm is genuine and contagious. People like to be around them.

Let's say you are selling what we usually think is a drab product— perhaps electronic equipment. Now, what people will tell you they care about most is, "Will it work and is the price good?" Until recently, most computers were packaged in functional, not especially attractive, gray boxes. Most computers looked pretty much the same.

But then Apple Computers did something that helped its computers fly off the shelves. Apple started putting its computers in attractive brightly-colored boxes. Apple changed the packaging of its computers. Apple theorized that people not only wanted their computer to work, they also want their computers to look good, to look hip. Computers today have become a form of jewelry. When people take their laptops out at Starbucks to start typing away, they want their computers to look cool, snazzy, zippy, high tech. Even the appearance of electronic equipment counts and can dramatically affect sales. Apple tapped into the "feelings" side of the brain.

How do you do this in print?

All kinds of ways.

You can do it with a challenge, perhaps even vaguely insulting your reader:

> "When are you finally going to get tired enough of being fat to do something about it?"

This will certainly create an emotional response, and might be the right approach for selling gym memberships.

Here's another approach:

> Three years ago I buried my eight-year old son Jimmy.
>
> He was killed when he got his hands on a neighbor's handgun that was not properly stored and locked. The gun was loaded, went off, and killed my son.
>
> I have dedicated the last three years of my life to developing a gun safe that

can only be opened with a handprint --
the handprint of the owner of the gun.

I am not at all anti-gun.

I believe strongly in the Second
Amendment. But I also believe that with
rights come responsibilities. We gun
owners have a duty to make sure our guns
are stored safely.

I am convinced that this safe can make
gun-owner homes safe homes for children,
and will help prevent more tragedies,
such as happened in our family.

Can you see how an approach like this does not rely on hype and screaming at the reader?

Emotion is created by the details, the facts, and the story. Note also that the writer is very clear that he is not anti-gun-owner—essential when selling a product to gun-owners.

Skillful story telling, with carefully selected and choreographed details to generate emotion, cause your reader to pay close attention, and set the stage for getting the order.

Chapter Twenty-Five
Seven words or less

Approach all your sales letter writing with this thought in mind.

If you can't sum up your basic message in one seven-word (or shorter) sentence, your letter is probably doomed. You should ask yourself, "Can I fit my central message on a bumper sticker?" If not, stop writing. You'll be wasting your time and money.

The people you're writing to are very busy. They receive a lot of mail every day. They're thinking about things other than the product or service you're writing about. You need to get their attention. If you can't convey your message or offer in about three seconds, your letter is headed for the circular file. Don't ask your reader to try to figure out what you're trying to say.

You must be able to convey your main message instantly with headlines, on your reply form, in your P.S., and in the first sentence of your letter. These are the places your readers will glance at first to decide whether they should keep reading, or pitch your letter in the trash.

Chapter Twenty-Six
Long versus short letters

Testing shows that long letters usually work better than short letters. This is yet another example of how direct mail is "counter-intuitive."

Common sense would seem to dictate that short letters would work better. Who has time to read a four-page or eight-page letter?

But testing consistently shows otherwise. Long works far better than short 80 percent of the time. A four-page letter will work better than a two-page letter. An eight-page letter will work better than a four-page letter.

This is a general rule. There are, of course, exceptions.

The reason is this: About half the people who answer your letter with a contribution or order will have read every word. The other half who answer will have scanned your appeal. The scanners read the first line, the P.S. and the reply form, your headlines and perhaps some of your underlined phrases. Your scanners don't need a long letter.

But half your buyers want all the information before they make a decision to buy. These people can't get enough information. And if you fail to answer all their questions, they won't buy. You must write for both audiences: Your scanners as well as those who can't get enough information.

Of course, there comes a point of diminishing returns. A 16-page letter is overkill in most cases, and may drive your cost up too high, though I have written a number of very successful 16-page letters. The fact that it's 16 pages is enough to get a reader's attention, and suggests that the writer must have a lot of important things to say. Generally, a 16-page letter will out-pull an eight-page letter, but maybe not enough to make up for the increased cost.

But there are important exceptions to this rule. Subscription and membership renewal notices should be short and look more like invoices than letters. A one- or two-page letter works best here and also keeps your cost lower.

If the service, product, or cause does not need much explaining, a short letter will work best. A dentist might send you a reminder that it's been more than six months since your last check-up. No need, in this case, for this notice to include a long letter describing all his services.

If the President of the United States is writing to his supporters asking for contributions for his reelection campaign, he does not need a long letter. The need is obvious. It does not require explaining. Everyone knows who the President of the United States is. Everyone knows political campaigns cost money. Besides, a Presidential election is in the news everyday. In a case like this, a long letter will be a distraction and likely depress contributions.

Credit card offers are usually short. Everyone knows what a credit card is for and who the major credit card companies are. All that needs to be explained is the offer. What is the interest rate? What is the annual fee? What are some of the incentives and benefits? This job can be done on one or two pages.

Long letters will almost always work best in prospecting. Since, in a prospect letter you are writing to people who have never bought anything from you and know nothing about you, more explaining will be needed to persuade your reader to try your service.

Your letters to those who have already bought something from you can be a mix of long and short letters, whatever is appropriate. The length of your letter should be determined by how much you have to say. The rule is to answer all the questions your reader might have. If this requires eight pages, write eight pages; if it requires four, write four.

Don't waste words. Make the message simple and compelling. Don't bore your reader. Pull the reader through the copy. The easiest step a reader can take is to stop reading and go on to something else. Your reader will know if you're not saying anything of much importance.

Every word should count. Every word, every phrase, every sentence should have a purpose. All superfluous words and sentences should be ruthlessly cut. But don't cut copy just to make your letter fit on two pages or four pages either. Tell the whole story.

But there's another side benefit of the long letter. A very long letter, eight pages or more, is attention-getting in itself. It adds weight and heft to your package. Kind of makes your #10 envelope, stuffed full of paper, feel like a brick when it arrives in the mailbox. "I wonder what's in here," your readers will ask themselves.

Don't write an 8- or 12- or 16-page letter just to do it. Make certain you really have enough to say to fill up all this paper. But the attention-getting aspect of a very long letter is a factor to consider. Many of my most successful direct mail packages land with a thud when dropped on a kitchen table.

Chapter Twenty-Seven
The all-important start of your letter

The first line is the most important line in the letter—in fact, in the entire package. I will sometimes think for hours, even days about the all-important first line.

If I have the right first line, very often the rest of the letter is easy to write. It almost seems to write itself. Every sentence flows so easily if you've started with the right first sentence.

You know you've chosen the wrong first sentence if the rest of the letter proves difficult to write. In fact, if your letter is difficult to write, chances are it will be difficult for your reader to understand. You should probably just stop writing and go back to the drawing board.

The first sentence is like the foundation upon which you build a house. If the foundation is wrong, the entire structure will collapse.

The all-important job of the first sentence is to interest your reader enough that she continues to read the next sentence, and then hopefully the entire letter. Your first sentence must be so captivating that it's more difficult to stop reading than to keep reading.

That's no easy task.

Here are some approaches I use:

1) The damaging admission

```
    If an idiot like me can write ads that
take in more than $50,000, then I'm betting
you can too.
```

```
    If a person of average intelligence like
me can earn $400,000 a year sitting in my
boxer shorts on the couch tapping away on my
laptop computer keyboard, I'll bet you can
too.
```

```
    I have never been more upset with myself
than when I started reading this book.

    That's because I now know I have wasted
half of my working life pursuing a
completely wrong approach to my business and
professional life.

    But the good news is it was not too late
to change my approach.
```

```
    I have not had much success working with
Fortune 500 companies.

    That's because I have little patience
with meetings, bureaucracy, and the snail-
like pace at which decisions are made.
```

How To Write...

I work best with entrepreneurs and small business people who are as impatient as I am, and who demand immediate results.

2) A startling, frightening statement

If your child is still lagging behind his peers in school by the fourth grade, he will likely lag behind his peers for the rest of his life.

Now is the time to take action if you think your child is falling behind.

* * * *

If you are 15 pounds overweight, the odds are your life will be 10 years shorter.

3) The proposition

- "If you will give me just 30 minutes of your time a month, I will show you how to double your income in less than a year."

- "If you are a non-smoker, you can save 50% a year on life insurance."

- "If your firm needs temporaries, we'll give you your first temp for free."

- "If you've written a book, we'll show you how to get it published."

- "If you'll give me a few minutes of your time, I'll show you how to collect from Social Security no matter what your age."

4) A question that engages the reader

- "If I could show you how you can add 20 yards to your drive in just six swings, would you be interested?"

- "Did you know there are still some people who do not know that...?"

- "Do you fear public speaking?"

5) A question that puts your reader on the spot

- "How much do you love your family? Enough to make sure they are financially secure in the event something happens to you?"

- "Are you ashamed of the smells in your kitchen?

- "Are you embarrassed to try for high-paying jobs because of your poor vocabulary?"

- "What step will you take first if your profits drop this year by 15%?"

- "Are you respected by your employees, or do they laugh at you behind your back?"

- "Does your low income embarrass you?"

6) Breaking news

- "I have just finished attending a conference of the world's leading oncologists, and I have some news for you about the latest treatments for cancer."

- "Because of your excellent credit rating, we are raising your credit limit to $25,000."

- "Congratulations! You have been admitted to Harvard."

7) The mysterious preview

"If you will just give me six minutes of your time and read my entire letter, I expect it will be the most profitable six minutes of your life."

8) Reliance on experts

- "What do doctors use when they have headaches?"

- "What does Tiger Woods do when his swing goes off track?"

- "As the team doctor for the New York Yankees, _____ is what I give the players for their muscle aches."

9) Rooting for the underdog

- "They laughed when they saw me strap on a snowboard, but not when they saw me come down the mountain like a pro."

- "They chuckled when I volunteered to test my skills against my judo teacher, but their laughs turned to amazement when he was lying on the mat."

10) Riveting story that can be told instantly

"Three years ago, my wife died of lung cancer. Had I known what I know now, she would still be alive."

11) Bestow honor

- "Congratulations! Because of your outstanding record as a_____, you have been awarded..."

- "Because of your excellent credit rating, you are among a handful of people who are being awarded a Platinum Card."

12) Prestigious invitation

- "Congratulations!

  Because of your exemplary academic record at Jefferson High School, you have been nominated by your teacher, Mrs. Joan Smith, to be a delegate to the National Young Leaders Conference in Washington, D.C. this fall."

- "Because you are a key leader in law enforcement, you are invited to participate in the White House Conference on Counter-Terrorism."

- "Congressman Jim Smith requests the honor of your presence at _____ ."

13) Free gift incentive to act now

- "I have two tickets to the Yankees-Red Sox game for you, but I'll need to know by Tuesday if you can use them."

- "You've won a free trip for two to Las Vegas. It includes non-stop airfare and two nights at the spectacular Mirage hotel. All you have to do is call by Thursday, May 23, to pick up your e-tickets and hotel reservation confirmation number."

14) Attention-getting enclosure

- "I have enclosed this $1 bill both to get your attention for my letter and to highlight how much it will cost you to become a 21st Century Broadband home for 60 days."

- "I have enclosed this free DVD for you because I knew you would not otherwise believe your son can learn the fundamentals of baseball in just seven days at my camp."

- "I am sending you this $10,000 check made payable to RST that will allow you to pay for your first mailing with RST."

- "I am sending you a free signed copy of my new book which I hope you will read before you arrive at my seminar on October 12."

- "I have enclosed a check in the amount of your first month's car payment. Just bring it to me before August 1 for your free test drive of the new _____."

15) Action and involvement

- "If you will complete the enclosed survey and mail it back to me by July 3, I will send you my new book."

- "You have been specially selected to participate in the enclosed survey for Congress on the threat of..."

- "I hope you have the courage to Test your I.Q. online by going to IQTest.com to see if you might qualify to..."

- "I encourage you to complete the enclosed application to see if you might qualify to enroll in The Screenplay Writers Institute."

Notice that many of these sentences combine techniques and strategies, and could be put in more than one of these categories.

To write powerful leads, first, tap into as many emotions and desires as you possibly can. Then get to, or at least hint at, what you are offering or the opportunity you are presenting, while at the same time creating enough intrigue and mystery so that your reader has little choice but to keep reading.

Can you see how none of these leads scream at the reader?

These leads are all factual, no empty hype like "I have an incredible offer for you."

Empty hype words like "incredible" and "amazing" are, in fact, the quickest way to ensure your reader stops reading.

If you always keep in mind that your readers are as smart, or smarter than you are, you will have a far greater chance of success.

Chapter Twenty-Eight
Your best lead sentence might be on page three

Once I finish writing the first draft of my letter, I will put it aside. I will then come back later to search for the very best line in the letter—which might be buried on page two or page three.

Why is this?

I think it's because great lines often come in a flash of inspiration. They come out almost on their own in the midst of a writing frenzy. They come when you are not really trying. I'll sometimes read a line I wrote and can't believe I wrote something so good. The rest of the letter might be garbage, probably is. But that one line is a diamond in the rough.

Another reason is that when we copywriters sit down to write, we write because we have to. We have no choice. It's how we make our living and pay our mortgage. If we don't write, we don't eat.

We will sit there staring at the blank computer screen. We can either sit there or write. I usually write, because then I feel I am at least doing something. But that does not mean what I am writing is any good.

But for me the mere process of writing forces me to start thinking. The more I write, the more the pieces of my argument start falling into place. And then I will find that key piece of the puzzle in the pile that will form the cornerstone for completing the project. The entire letter and package will flow once I figure out what the key piece is—what the key sentence is.

So when you've finished your first draft, your work has just begun. Now you must scour your draft for your very best sentence, your very best point.

Other writers work very differently from me. Other writers are highly organized. They make an outline before they write. Then they follow the outline. I'm sure that works for some, maybe most. But outlines don't work for me.

I'm a stream-of-consciousness writer. What I do is dump all my very best ideas and thoughts on my computer keyboard. I write page after page of thoughts and ideas. I then go back and organize it and assemble it. My first draft is more like shapeless clay. Once I've created the clay, I then get out my chisel and start sculpting.

Chapter Twenty-Nine
Get to the point immediately

Has a salesman ever come to your door and stood there talking with you for minutes without saying why he's there?

He asks you how you are doing. He talks about the weather. He comments on how nice your house is and how nice your kids are. You then finally ask, "What are you selling?"...if you haven't slammed the door in his face with an "I'm not interested."

The reality is, as soon as your readers open your envelope and see your letter, they instantly know they are being pitched—sold something. And they won't give you more than about three seconds to figure out what you've got to sell. They aren't going to read a page or two to find out what your pitch is about.

They'll judge it by the first sentence.

James Bond movies always start with a great action sequence. Never will a James Bond movie start with a long-winded conversation. Opera fans do not go to operas to hear singers clear their throats. They go for the performance.

Your readers want the performance to start with the first sentence.

Chapter Thirty
The power of the word "mistake"

The word "mistake" has the magic quality of making whatever it is you are saying more interesting.

If you say, "Let me tell you about a serious mistake I made that cost me a lot of money," ears will immediately perk up.

Would you rather listen to someone boast about his great achievements? Or would you rather listen to someone talk about his own mistakes as a way to help you avoid making the same mistakes?

How To Write...

People also want to hear about costly mistakes they might be making.

Try incorporating the word "mistake" into your lead sentences and headlines, and see what happens. Here are a few ideas you might borrow:

- "Have you made any of these investment mistakes?"

- "Don't make this mistake when choosing someone to fix your roof"

- "Would you like to identify and correct the single biggest mistake in your golf swing in just 10 minutes?"

- "Are you among the 90% of parents who make this same mistake when talking to your children?"

- "Here's a mistake I'll bet you're making every day in your marriage."

- "Here's one mistake I hope you never make with your career."

- "Here are the 10 most common mistakes surgeons make in the operating room."

- "I made a big mistake in not writing to you sooner."

- "Let me tell you about the biggest marketing mistake I made that cost me a lot of money and nearly bankrupted me. I don't want you to make the same mistake."

- "I made a serious mistake. I apologize."

People love hearing about mistakes. But using the word "mistake" is especially powerful when talking about your own mistakes.

"For years I was making the same mistakes
in my workout and exercise routine. Even
though I was going to the gym four times a
week, I couldn't figure out why I wasn't
getting any stronger. And then I
discovered..."

You might then follow this introduction with these kinds of questions: "Does this sound familiar? Are any of you making this same mistake?"

I'm sure you've noticed that the best way to diffuse your customer or client's anger with you is to immediately admit your mistake, following up with an apology. Something along these lines: "I apologize for my mistake. As my way to try to make amends, I have enclosed two tickets for the New York Giants football game."

When a baseball manager apologizes for making a comment that could be interpreted as racist; when he goes on TV and says, "I am truly sorry for my mistake. It was a very stupid choice of words. I did not intend to hurt anyone," people sympathize with the poor fellow who has just been fired from his job. They forgive him if he admits his mistake.

My banker recently made a big mistake with my money. I had asked him to transfer a sizeable sum of money by wire to one of my mailshops. He transferred the wrong amount, adding an extra zero.

Yikes!

The money went out.

When I ran into the bank in a panicked frenzy because my entire bank account had been drained, and pointed out the error, the banker made the mistake of trying to blame me for his mistake. He said, "That's what you told me to send"...even though the written record of the transaction had the correct amount.

Everyone makes mistakes. I was far less annoyed with his mistake than I was by his effort to try to blame me (the customer!) for his mistake. All he had to say was, "I'm very sorry for my mistake. I'll get the money back into your account immediately."

Talk about a really bad sales tactic!

The word "mistake" has many uses. It's a powerful word to keep in mind for all your marketing and customer relations efforts.

The word helps establish your credibility and trustworthiness. It's an almost magic word that automatically makes whatever you're saying worth listening to.

Chapter Thirty-One
You can't sell by boring your reader

Fascinating facts, shocking details, riveting narratives keep people listening and reading.

People aren't going to watch a boring movie or finish reading a boring book. The easiest next step for any reader to take is to stop reading and to go onto something else.

Facts and statistics leave everyone cold. What people want is flesh and blood—human stories. *People* magazine, *National Inquirer,* and *Star* are popular publications because they report gossip on famous people. People are interested in people.

In your opinion, which of the following is the stronger way to communicate your point?

> "350,000 people die of cancer every year."

Or...

> "I'm sending you a photo of my little eight-year-old friend, Jimmy, who died of cancer today."

Reciting statistics and numbers is death in direct mail sales copy. Statistics are impersonal. It's one thing to say six million Jews died in the Holocaust. It's quite another to watch *Schindler's List*, read the *Diary of Anne Frank,* or visit the Holocaust Museum in Washington, D.C., where you will see, hear, read, and feel the stories of actual people.

Statistics leave no impression on the brain. Statistics leave the reader uninvolved.

Now you may want to include a few statistics in your direct mail letter to back up some of your claims. And sometimes statistics can be interesting if they are especially shocking or surprising. But usually not.

Your letter certainly does need to appeal to the brain part of your reader, not just to triggering emotions. But statistics and numbers will not move your reader to buy, or even to read further. A stunning story about a real person will. The right story about an actual person will pull your reader into your presentation.

Copy aimed at the heart will always out-pull copy aimed at the mind. Jesus knew this. He used parables, stories that made his points. He did not approach us with data. He did not say 3,000,000 people went to Hell today—though that statement might certainly have gotten the riveted and focused attention of his audience! Remember, your goal is not to win a debate with your readers. Your goal is to move the emotion or impulse side of the brain in such a way that they will buy.

But if you feel you absolutely must use a statistic in your letter to show the magnitude of the problem, try something like this:

```
    Imagine if the September 11 attack on
America happened 100 times a year.

    Imagine terrorists flying planes into
our buildings, killing 3,000 people twice
a week.

    That's exactly what cancer is doing:
killing 6,000 people every single week.
```

This is far more powerful than simply saying "350,000 people die of cancer every year," because here you are connecting a number to an actual event you know your reader has experienced. You are giving meaning to the number. September 11 was a shocking event for every American. It was an emotional event.

Now you are pointing out that cancer causes just as catastrophic an event more than 100 times a year, every year. By connecting your pitch to an event like what happened on September 11, a catastrophic event we all experienced, you are providing a graphic visual image of the horrifying carnage cancer leaves in its wake each day. You are tapping into your reader's emotions. You are getting your reader involved, in a personal way, to show the magnitude of the crisis you are writing about.

You can then go into your program for how your reader can avoid this catastrophe in her life.

How To Write...

Chapter Thirty-Two
The P.S.

After your reader has read the first line of your letter, the next place she'll likely look is the P.S.

In fact, many people read the P.S. first, because they know that's where they will find the bottom line of why you're writing to them.

The P.S. summarizes the action you want your reader to take and restates the offer. Try not to simply repeat lines from the letter, but don't depart from your theme either. Keep the P.S. short and to the point.

Remind the reader of the need for the immediate arrival of the check, order, or reservation. I always include a deadline date for the order and explain the reason for the deadline. The P.S. should also remind the reader about the money-back guarantee.

The P.S. is a great place to offer your reader instant gratification by providing a toll-free 1.800 number and an online order option so your reader can order immediately and perhaps have the product delivered overnight.

Chapter Thirty-Three
Headlines

Headlines are absolutely essential for grabbing the attention of your reader. Headlines are what people read to see if they have any interest in what you have to say.

The headline writers at the *New York Post* and *National Inquirer* are masters of the craft. People buy these newspapers entirely because of the headlines. And people read the articles because they want the details that justify such amazing headlines.

Headline writing is critical in all sales and marketing copy. Here are some fill-in-the-blank headline formulas you might find useful.

**"21 rules for writing headlines
that sell"**

**"Seven predictions for 2008 that can change
your life"**

"Eleven secrets of successful investing"

"I lost 10 pounds in 10 days"

**"How moving to Nevada saved my
company $1,000,000 the first year"**

**"How I slashed $50,000 off my
income tax bill"**

**"How I'm able to spend my day at the
office in the nude"**

**"Why I'll never let my kids sit
in a classroom"**

"The biggest mistake made by parents"

**"Why my 10-year old boy would rather read
a book than watch TV"**

**"How I beat cancer by knowing what
questions to ask my doctor"**

**"How I solved my sex problems without
Viagra or any other drug"**

How To Write...

**"How I put excitement back
in my marriage"**

**"How I got my wife to stop nagging me and
start praising me"**

**"How I motivated myself to
get in shape"**

**"How you can look like this and never
lift a weight"**

**"If you like to write, I can teach
you how to make $30,000 a month from home"**

"WARNING:_____"

**"WARNING: 138,000 middle managers just
like you will lose their jobs by 2008"**

**"WARNING: The company you work for has
already spent your retirement"**

**"WARNING: You probably will be sued for
everything you're worth within the next 36
months"**

**"WARNING: The Stock Market
will drop 30%"**

"How to stop your divorce"

"How to double your dating"

"35 rules for staying in the lives of your kids when they grow up."

Can you see the pattern?

These headlines are aimed at hooking your reader.

Notice that nearly every one of these headlines taps into a fear or an anxiety people have. The word "secret" is an attention-getter.

People want secrets. I would like to know the secret to a consistent golf swing that will produce consistently straight shots. The word "hidden" is another word that triggers interest. People want to know where the "hidden" treasure is. Hidden implies almost no one knows about it. I just need a map. I just need someone to tell me where this "hidden" treasure is.

"How To..." and "How I..." are often good ways to start a headline. Also numbering the ways or items in your headline can be effective: "Seven Habits of Highly Effective People." A number suggests that the program is limited, definable, achievable. *If I do these seven things, I will be successful. I just need to complete the program,* are the thoughts we try to trigger here.

And notice, too, the headlines always create mystery and intrigue, telling the casual reader what the big benefit is without giving away any answers. The headline tells the reader, "Here's what this letter is about. But you'll need to read it to find the answer to your problem and to satisfy your desire."

By the way, your letter should include some actual answers.

Some professional direct mail sales letter writers make the mistake of having their entire letter be almost nothing but headlines and intriguing statements with no real answers.

Your letter does need to deliver the goods, or your reader will just be frustrated. Your reader will see you as just another skilled huckster, probably with nothing much of real value to offer.

Never be afraid to give away some of your product. Those who like it will want more. In addition, they will trust you.

Chapter Thirty-Four
Force an answer

Do everything in your creative power to get your reader to respond in some way.

Ask your reader to send back an answer to your letter—"Yes" or "No."

Asking for a response one way or the other requires the reader to make a decision. You want to give your reader reasons for needing to answer now—to make a decision.

The worst answer for a salesman is "I'll think about it and get back to you later." That means the answer is "no."

But the prospect is also keeping his options open. The easiest answer for your prospect to give is "maybe."

By requiring a "yes" or "no" answer on the spot, you are forcing your prospect to face a moment of truth. "If I answer no, I'll miss this opportunity forever" is the thought you must create in the mind of your prospect. The last thing you want your prospect to think is: "There's no hurry. There's no need for me to make a decision right now."

I've seen women take exactly this approach with men. "You either ask me to marry you now, or that's it. No more waiting. Tonight we will go out to dinner. If I don't have a ring on my finger by the end of dessert, I'm gone. Finito. You'll never see me again."

"Yikes!" the guy thinks. "I guess she's not going to let me string her along for another eight years. I better rush out and get that ring."

A weak salesman does not like to force this moment of truth, or require a "yes" or "no" answer on the spot. A weak salesman believes that if he does not get a "no" answer, he still has a chance to make the sale later.

Wrong.

He has very little chance of making any sales with this approach...because most people would rather never commit until they absolutely must. A strong salesman knows that forcing a moment of truth and requiring a decision on the spot will certainly produce more definitive "no" answers. But he will also force many more "yes" answers—many more sales.

There are many methods of forcing the decision. You might say in the P.S. "If you decide not to subscribe, would you mind writing me a note telling me why?" Or, "If you decide not to subscribe, please just write 'I am not subscribing' across the order form and mail it back to me. That way I will know you received and read my letter, and I won't bother you again."

I'm sure you've seen the "Yes" and "No" sticker on offers that come through the mail. The marketer here is trying to force you to make a "yes" or "no" decision.

I'm not a big fan of these stickers. They don't look like a real moment of truth to me. But that's the effect these marketers are attempting to create in the minds of their readers.

In a fundraising solicitation I mailed, I asked supporters of the organization to return the booklet of "Monthly Gift coupons" and the accompanying "set of 12 reply envelopes" if they had decided **not** to participate in the monthly giving program I was promoting.

Many of those who elected to return the booklets included a one-time gift. Many of those who returned the booklets were too embarrassed to do so with no gift at all.

So in all your mailings, always think of ways to require a response one way or the other—to force a decision.

Chapter Thirty-Five
The Johnson Box

This is really just another form of headline.

A Johnson Box is a line or two of copy depicted in a box-shaped outline of asterisks or a tinted box. Its purpose is to highlight text that conveys the key message of the direct mail offer. The Johnson Box appears between the salutation and letterhead.

Usually the text is in Courier type, just like the rest of the letter. But sometimes it is bold or red and the lines might be centered instead of left justified.

The text in a Johnson Box is generally longer than the usual headline. Instead of a flat statement, it might be a proposition. It might be more like a lead sentence.

The Johnson Box was named after its developer, a famous copywriter named Frank Johnson. He was a copywriter for *Time*, and *American Heritage*, and spent the latter part of his life as a consultant and freelance copywriter on many highly successful direct marketing projects. Johnson passed away in 2001 at the age of 88.

I've developed a variation some of my copywriting peers call "The Hart Preface"...which is similar to a Johnson Box, but a bit longer. While a "Johnson Box" contains a statement or proposition more akin to a headline, my own "Hart Preface" might contain two sentences that span four to six lines. It's a kind of mini-letter—much like the "summaries" you see at the start of articles in *U.S. News and World Report*.

The principle is: summarize the article in an intriguing way and entice the browser, the skimmer, to dive into the full article.

Chapter Thirty-Six

The longer you hold your reader's attention, the better your odds of getting the sale

The car salesman wants to keep you in the showroom. He knows that if you leave the showroom, the chance he will ever get the sale is near nil.

If your reader puts your letter aside, thinking "I'll come back to it later" you can be near 100% certain she will never be back. If she ever comes back, it's a bonus.

On the other hand, if you can write in such a way that captivates your reader (like Stephen King writes), you have a great chance of getting the sale. The longer your prospect reads, the better chance you have of getting the order.

There is only one reason your prospect will continue reading your letter: You are striking a chord with your reader. What you are saying is of intense interest to your reader. Your reader will continue to read only if it's more difficult for your reader to stop reading than to continue reading...because what you are saying is so fascinating.

The sales letter writer's job is <u>not</u> to write

The sales writer's job is not to write any more than the car salesman's job is to talk. The car salesman's job is to sell cars.

Your job is not to dazzle your reader with your writing skill. Your job is not to impress your reader with your big vocabulary or your intelligence. Your job is not to tell your reader fascinating stories. Your job is not to amuse your reader.

Your job is to get and keep your reader's attention and to present arguments and reasons so compelling that your reader sends a check or picks up the phone to call with credit card in hand.

Your job is to sell.

Chapter Thirty-Seven
The difference between letters to business executives and mass-market letters to consumers

Whether writing to the business executive trying to land the big consulting contract, or selling a newsletter subscription to a consumer, the structure of your arguments are essentially the same.

You still need headlines in your proposal, or sales pitch. You still need to assemble a "show-and-tell presentation." Business executives are very busy people. Just like the mass-market consumer, if they can't grasp what you are selling, what you are proposing, in about three seconds or less, you're gone, finito, out the door, never to be seen or heard from again.

The busy, self-important business executive won't give you a second chance—unlike the far more forgiving consumer.

So bore the business executive at your own peril.

But there are clearly some important differences.

If you are selling a high-end product or service to a big successful business, you must come across as highly professional. No offset "Dear Friend" letters here.

You must send business executives letters that look like they are from one person to another—personalized, highly-individualized, business-style letters. Instead of the 50 cents per letter you might spend on consumer offers, you might spend $5 or more on a letter and proposal to a business. Your letter and proposal should arrive with first-class postage (not bulk) and perhaps even via FedEx. And the paper you use should be nice bond, perhaps even watermark paper—a quality paper that communicates excellence. Successful business executives want to do business with other successful people. They have no time or patience to meet with a salesman who has holes in his shoes and whose suit doesn't fit.

As in all direct marketing, your presentation must fit the audience. If you are writing to the chairman of GM, make sure your presentation appears worthy of reading. Make sure it does not look like junk mail. Cut no corners, spare no expense here.

And there will be some differences in language. You will need to be more measured in your approach. You will need to sound like a successful executive talking to another successful executive.

But other than these relatively cosmetic differences, the structure of your presentation and offer can and should follow the same basic principles. Remember, human nature is a constant. Whether you are rich or poor, you have the same basic motivations. You have fears and frustrations and problems—whether you live in a trailer park or are the Chairman of GM.

Some of the details of your specific problems will certainly be different. But the rich man and the poor man are still worried about basically the same things. They both worry about money, about legal issues, about the future, about all those sharks circling in the water waiting to devour them, and about all the threats to their well-being that are always out there.

So you still use exactly the same rules of marketing when you are talking with the business executive and the mass-market consumer. You just make sure you change your clothes and adjust your language depending on your audience. You should not talk the same way to longshoremen as you do to college professors. In all marketing, you must learn and speak the language of those you are talking to.

But the same fundamental principles of marketing always apply. For example...

I once made a decision to try enclosing a $1 bill in a proposal I was sending to a wealthy business executive.

I was urged by my copywriting peers not to do that. "There's just no way a multi-millionaire, a graduate of Harvard business school no less, will respond to a $1 bill package. He will see it as a gimmick and pitch it in the trash."

"Not if I say up front that enclosing this $1 bill is a gimmick," I answered. "Not if we tell our Harvard-educated multimillionaire reader that the purpose of enclosing this $1 bill is to get the attention of a busy executive."

My letter started this way:

```
Dear Mr. Smith:

    I have taken the very usual step of
enclosing a $1 bill in a clear plastic
envelope for a reason.

    I had to think of a way to get your
attention for my letter, to make sure my
letter stood out in your mail.

    I would never do something this gimmicky
if I were not writing to you about an
important matter to you and your company.

    But I am a marketing professional. That's
how I make my living.

    And I have found in more than 19 years
of experience that enclosing a $1 bill
with my letter, especially if it arrives
in a clear plastic envelope, almost always
increases response to my sales and
marketing letters by 50% or more.

    Mr. Smith, I believe I have a way to
significantly improve your marketing,
perhaps improve your return on investment
```

on all your marketing efforts by 50% or
more if you will give me a few minutes of
your time.

I would like to come in and meet with
you to talk about your marketing.

I have scores of methods and techniques
that I use, besides enclosing $1 bills
with my letters, that will ensure your
letters and your marketing materials are
opened and read by your target audience.

In the next few days, I will call your
secretary, Linda Johnson, to see if I can
meet with you in the next week or two.

My hope is that you will let Ms.
Johnson know so she will expect my call.
Alternatively, you may have her call me to
schedule the appointment.

My direct office number is _____.
If she can't reach me there, my cell phone
number is _____.

Guess what happened.

My mailing that included a $1 bill as a gimmick to get the
attention of my reader worked even better to the wealthy, highly-
educated business executive than to ordinary consumers.

Why? Because, in truth, a wealthy person will pay attention to
something interesting just as any mass-market consumer will.

Do wealthy people go to the same movies as regular people? Yes,
they do...because they also like to see a good movie. They will also
pay attention to a letter that arrives in unusual packaging and will
listen to an attractive offer.

But you will also notice that with this letter I invested a great deal of
time, effort, and expense in personalization when writing to this wealthy
prospect. And I could afford to because the potential payoff was so big.

For example, the letter specifically mentions the name of his
secretary. Getting this information requires some individualized
legwork. You won't be able to get this information by renting a

compiled list from Dun & Bradstreet. You will need to find this kind of personalized information on your own.

The look, feel, and tone of the letter is very important when writing to a business executive. A salesman is far more likely to make a sale to a successful business executive if the clothes of the salesman and his style of speaking look and sound right. The same is true for your letter.

Chapter Thirty-Eight
Short words, short sentences, short paragraphs

I try to make every sentence a stand-alone headline that explains itself. That's not always possible. But it's a goal I strive for. Use short declarative sentences.

When you select words, choose the shortest one. Instead of "allow" choose "let." Instead of "prevent" use the word "stop" if the shorter word will work just as well.

Avoid four-syllable words whenever possible. Avoid unusual words (no Latin or French phrases).

Write in plain English. I'm not happy if I see paragraphs more than three lines in length in a sales letter.

Generally, one sentence per paragraph is enough. I often use one-word paragraphs, like "Why?" and "How?"...or brief phrases as entire paragraphs, such as "Please let me explain."

These very short paragraphs help break up the copy and make your letter "scannable" and easy on the eyes. Short paragraphs help keep the reader moving through your letter.

Your reader is far more likely to keep reading your letter if your letter is easy to read.

Your language should be direct. Avoid multi-clause sentences. Short declarative sentences are far more powerful. Ernest Hemmingway understood this.

Most writers don't.

Chapter Thirty-Nine
42 magic phrases that will help every writer of sales letters

1. "Congratulations!"

2. "Frankly, I'm puzzled."

3. "To order, just use the postage-paid reply envelope I've enclosed for your convenience. Or, to receive your _____ within 48 hours, just call 1.800._____ right now or order online by going to **www.websiteorderform.com**."

4. "And there's no risk to you because if you are not completely satisfied in every way, just return your _____ and I'll send you a full refund, no questions asked."

5. "But before I explain further, please let me introduce myself. My name is _____ and I am President of _____."

6. "You are cordially invited to..."

7. "You have been nominated by [familiar name] to become a member of _____."

8. "In looking over our records, I noticed that..."

9. "Did you know that...?"

10. "Here are some examples of what you will find in..."

11. "For example,..."

12. "If you will just give me just six minutes of your time right now, I will show you how..."

13. "The registration deadline is..."

14. "I have already covered the postage on your reply envelope so you would not need to waste any time hunting for a stamp."

15. "Just one idea that you get from this newsletter will be worth many, many times the price of your subscription."

16. "Let me list here 39 reasons why you should..."

17. "Don't read this unless you've decided <u>not</u> to order."

18. "As soon as your order arrives on my desk, I will immediately..."

19. "I won't cash your check or process your credit card payment for 30 days until I know you are completely happy with..."

20. "If a person of very average intelligence like me can...then surely you will have no difficulty..."

21. "Send no money."

22. "Like you, I'm..."

23. "If you're like me, you probably..."

24. "I will anxiously look for your reply to arrive on my desk in the next few days."

25. "I look forward to talking with you about this in more detail when we meet."

26. "If you have any questions or would like to discuss this further, please feel free to give me a call. My direct office number is _____. I'll also give you my cell phone number, which is _____."

27. "I know this sounds too good to be true, which is why I want you to try it for 30 days before I send you the invoice."

28. "So that's why..."

29. "Because..."

30. "Better yet..."

31. "Why? Because..."

32. "As a Charter Member, you will lock in these low rates for the next..."

33. "Not available anywhere else."

34. "More important..." and "Most important..."

35. "Or, if you prefer..."

36. "I know from your past activities that you are..."

37. "Your colleague, _____, gave me your name because he thought you..."

38. "You have been specially selected to participate in the enclosed National Survey of..."

39. "You can send your check today or, if you prefer, I'll send you a bill later."

40. "I am writing to apologize..."

41. "I have made an error."

42. "I am sending you these two free tickets to _____ because..."

Chapter Forty

The importance of "scannability"

Your letter, in fact your entire package, must be "scannable"—easy on the eye, with no large blocks of intimidating text. There's no greater stopper for a reader than to see a large block of undifferentiated text on the page.

Yuck!

Use bullets when you have a list of points. Use indented paragraphs in bold to set certain paragraphs apart from others. Use sub-headlines throughout your letter—lots of sub-heads if your letter is long. Decide what the most important paragraph in your letter is, place it on the first page, and print it as an indented block paragraph in red.

When you use an indented block paragraph for emphasis, keep it all on one page. Don't start it near the bottom of the page so it continues on the next page, or you'll destroy the effect. It will just look odd. It's best if your indented block paragraphs are near the middle of the page, so it pops out at the reader.

Underlining key phrases in your letter will help catch the eyes of your readers and keep them reading. But don't underline too many phrases, or your underlining will lose its impact.

Think of underlining as similar to headline writing. The phrases you underline should be mini-headlines. Your reader should be able to understand your entire offer by reading only the underlined phrases, usually sentence fragments, hardly ever entire sentences.

Other graphic devices include:

1. Numbering items in a list.

2. Boxes.

3. Handwritten blue notes in margins.

4. Handwritten brackets alongside paragraphs you want to draw attention to.

5. Red type in the body of your letter.

6. Lines and boxes made of asterisks **************

7. Screens (washes of light color over a block of text you want to set apart).

8. Wrap Courier text of the letter around a photo.

9. Be sure all photos have captions.

10. Varied type. Sometimes my Courier letter will change to a blue handwritten font.

I once used this last device (#10 on the above list) when writing a letter to ad agencies as a way to demonstrate the capabilities of RST Marketing—a great mailshop I use for my high-end, highly personalized, high-impact mailings.

All these graphic devices make a long letter easier and more inviting to read. They help a long letter read like a short letter.

And the use of these graphic devices should never be left up to the graphic artist, the typesetter, the mailshop, or someone else. The copywriter is the only person who can decide what, when, and how a graphic device is to be deployed.

Remember, the purpose of graphics is not to make the package look pretty; it's to strengthen the communication of your message. Only the copywriter can know what to emphasize, what points to draw the reader's attention to.

Once you've finished writing your letter and package, your job is only half done. You must then sit with your graphic artist and your production person (often for many hours) so that your package looks exactly the way you want it to look.

The graphics are an essential part of writing an effective direct mail sales letter and package.

Chapter Forty-One
Avoid "double stoppers"

Pages should not end with periods, if possible, especially on the first page.

Periods are stoppers and tend to cause people to stop reading. Periods, of course, are unavoidable. But a period at the end of the page creates a double stopper.

Microsoft Word is always forcing me to end pages with periods.

Ughhhh!

What a blunder. I'm always having to actively tell Microsoft Word (by taking the extra step of adding a page break) to stop ending my pages with periods. Periods and ends of pages are stop signs.

Ideally, you want a sentence that breaks and continues onto the next page to be especially gripping – like the TV miniseries that stops and says "To Be Continued..."

They always do this at the best part.

Stephen King is a master of this. He always ends chapters at an especially exciting juncture, often when someone is about to be killed.

Ellipses can help break up sentences and paragraphs and keep the reader's eyes moving through your letter.

The worst thing that can happen to a writer of sales letters is for your reader to stop reading. Use every trick in your arsenal to prevent this catastrophe—the catastrophe of your reader putting your letter aside and going on to something else.

Chapter Forty-Two
Get rid of "that"

In your direct mail letter, try to strike the word "that" from your sentences.

The word "that" is often unnecessary and usually weakens a sentence.

Comb your letters for the word "that" and strike it out whenever you can. Your sentences will immediately sound stronger and more direct. "Which" is another weak word you should avoid when possible in your direct mail letters.

You can't completely avoid using "that" and "which," but often these words are superfluous.

Sometimes, however, I will start a paragraph with the words "which" and "that's." This can be a useful transition device.

I'll sometimes start a paragraph by saying something like, "Which brings me to why I'm writing you today"; or "That's what I mean when I say..."

This can help keep your reader moving through your letter.

Chapter Forty-Three
Order forms

The order form is your moment of truth.

Will your reader pick it up and read it? Will she act on your offer?

Make your order form user friendly. Make it as easy as possible to fill out and order your product. The mistake people make in crafting order forms is to require too much information from the reader.

Many order forms I see (both on the Internet and that arrive in the mail) look like they were designed by the legal department or the accounting office, certainly not the marketing people.

Ask for the absolute bare minimum of information you need to process the order. Your order form should not frighten or turn off your reader. It should not look tedious, or be a chore to fill out.

Order forms should look like order forms.

All the information should appear exactly where your reader will expect to find it—not hidden somewhere, not in the fine print. I hate fine print (the product of lawyers) on order forms.

Make sure your customer can easily find out how much to write out a check for and who to write the check to. The money section is the most important section in the package. The money section is of intense interest to your reader. Make the money section easy to find, easy to read, and crystal clear.

A reply form should include an attention-getting headline that tells your customer what the offer is about.

The lead sentence, the P.S., and the reply form are places the reader looks first.

Of those who answer your letter, half will never read the entire letter. They will make their decision to contribute or buy based on the first line, the P.S., and what they see on the order form. Reply forms and order forms should contain all the action steps you want your reader to take.

Chapter Forty-Four
Make it easy to buy

Make it as easy as possible for your reader to order your product. You should use a postage-paid reply envelope—either include a business reply envelope or affix stamps to the reply envelope. You never want your reader to put your letter aside because she does not have a stamp readily at hand.

If it makes economic sense, I like affixing actual postage stamps to reply envelopes, rather than using the more customary BRE. Very few people will throw away an envelope with live stamps on it, totaling the first-class postage amount. To throw away this envelope is like throwing away money, even if the only way you can use these stamps is to mail back this reply envelope—which is exactly what you want your reader to do.

But don't just rely on people using the reply envelope to mail in a check with the order form filled out.

Include an option to pay by credit card, by phone, or online. Be sure to include a toll-free 1.800 number and the Web address for an online order form on all major components of your mailing. Be sure your 1.800 number and the URL for your online order form are easy to find.

No matter what component of your package your readers are holding, a way to order easily and instantly should be staring at them in the face...and prominently displayed.

Chapter Forty-Five
Keep it simple and clear

The instant your reader is confused by your sales presentation is the instant she will tune out.

Complexity is the enemy of sales.

In fact, complexity is the enemy of communication.

Sell just one thing. Ask for one decision, not many decisions with lots of options. Make your instructions clear, direct and easy to follow.

> Simple, clear sentences.
> Simple, clear action steps.
> Simple, clear order form.
> Simple, clear headlines.
> Simple, clear reasons.
> One simple, clear proposition.

Chapter Forty-Six
Have you heard the one about the guy who writes hilarious sales letters?

Humor is death to your sales letter.

Money is one of the most serious subjects in life. A salesman who dresses in a clown suit will not have much success. People don't buy from frivolous people. People don't buy from guys who wear funny ties or funny shoes.

Decisions to buy can be among the most anxiety-ridden decisions in life. These decisions produce cold sweats and sleepless nights, especially concerning life's big-ticket items.

Should I buy this house, or should I look some more? What if this car is a lemon? How do I know what stock to buy? Can I trust my stockbroker? Do I really need this expensive whole life insurance policy? How do I know if this is the right person to hire for this job? Do I really want to commit to a three-month consulting agreement with this guy? How do I know this is the right school for my child? Can I really afford this? How can I be sure I'm not being ripped off?

Do you want a surgeon who's funny? Do want a funny airline pilot? How about a funny car mechanic or a funny computer technician?

Jokes, uproarious laughter, and backslaps from the salesman will only increase your prospect's suspicion that he is being conned. This is just as true for your sales letter.

The job of your sales letter is not to amuse. The job of your sales letter is to reassure, to answer your reader's questions, to calm your reader's anxieties and suspicions.

Chapter Forty-Seven
How does your letter sound?

I **care much more how my letter** sounds than how it reads.

Because I know if it sounds good when I read it out loud, it will read well also.

I always read my letters out loud because I want my letters to sound the way people actually speak. I will read it out loud to others. I will have a child read it back to me out loud.

If a 10-year-old kid can read my letter back to me easily, and if my listeners can follow my letter easily by hearing it, if the letter flows smoothly when spoken, I know I'm on the right track.

I have never tried this, but I think I will. You would do well to take your letter to a bowling alley or maybe a neighborhood sports bar and read it to the folks there. Get their reaction. If their eyes glaze over, if they start looking around the room while you're reading, you'll know you must go back to the drawing board.

On the other hand, if some ask where they can get the product your letter is selling, you know you've probably written a winner.

Chapter Forty-Eight
Your zero-cost test mailing

Even relatively small test mailings of 5,000 or 10,000 letters will cost thousands of dollars and can cost a small fortune for a highly personalized, high-impact mailing with lots of elaborate inserts.

But here's another way to test your package before you've gone to all the expense of printing it.

Mock up your letter. Make it look exactly the way it will look when it's printed—or as close as possible. Your graphic artist can do this for you. And color laser printers today are able to make your components look like they are commercially produced.

Not only will you then be able to see how your package looks and feels before you've spent much money, but you will be able to test it on your wife, and perhaps your kids, your neighbors, and colleagues at the office.

First, address the mock-up you've created to your wife and put it in the mailbox, with all the other mail. And then watch carefully how your wife deals with it. Don't tell her it's a package you've created. Don't tell her what you're up to.

Does the package grab her attention? Does she miss it? Does she throw it in the trash or leave it in a pile with all the other junk mail. If the envelope grabs her attention and if she opens your sales letter, does she begin to read it? How much time does she spend on it? What does she read first? What does she skip?

Seeing how she responds to your package will tell you a lot about it.

After she's finished with it, ask her questions about it.

Again, for you to get her honest feedback, it's critical for her to have no idea it's your package. If she knows it's your creation, she'll just tell you how wonderful it is.

And don't get upset with her if your letter made little impact on her. Don't get mad if she was thoroughly unimpressed. Instead, thank her. She has just saved you a lot of money.

Try this same experiment with your kids, your neighbors, and colleagues at the office. If your package is making an impact, if the reaction looks positive, you can then feel better about your upcoming live test.

Chapter Forty-Nine
Ben's 24-hour rule

Once you've finished writing the first draft of your letter and reply form, put it away for at least twenty-four hours and then come back to it.

And then, when you read it through again after giving your weary brain a much-needed rest, see if it still reads as powerfully as you thought it did when you were writing it.

Writing is very difficult work, mentally exhausting. No writer can have an objective view of his own work until some time has passed and the memory of how hard you labored starts to fade. A day later, after a good night's sleep, your letter might not seem as good when you read it again with fresh eyes and a clear mind.

Ernest Hemmingway (my favorite writer) would finish a first draft of a novel and then throw it in a drawer. He would then go fishing or on a safari for six weeks and forget about the novel he had written. He would then return, refreshed, to begin his rewrites and edits. He needed at least six weeks away from the project in order to have a clear and objective mind when assessing the quality of his work.

We direct mail copywriters don't have the luxury of being able to wait six weeks between drafts of our letters. We are usually operating under tight deadlines. The client needs the copy yesterday.

But a minimum of twenty-four hours of rest between your drafts is required to honestly assess your work.

You know the old adage: "Never write a letter when angry and put it in the mail. It's okay to write a letter when angry, but throw it in a drawer and come back to it when your anger has subsided." The letter, when read with more dispassionate eyes, might sound pretty stupid a day later. "Where did that come from?" you might ask yourself.

I think the same rule applies with every writing project—and no less to a direct mail marketing piece where you have a lot of money riding on its success...or failure.

Chapter Fifty
Edit your letter ruthlessly

Once you come back to your letter after your 24-hour wait, prepare to edit your letter ruthlessly.

Cut out all superfluous sentences and words. Get rid of the passive voice and replace it with clear, active, direct, unambiguous statements. Strip out all empty hype words such as "incredible" and "amazing" and "best ever." Strike out all clichés.

Throw your weasel words in the garbage. Your readers are intelligent people. And they have become experts at detecting weasel words, which are really just lies.

Sometimes the lawyers force us to put weasel words in our copy. Lawyers are experts at weasel words. Try your best to avoid using them.

Edit for clarity and emotion. Strive to make each sentence a stand-alone headline that explains itself. Look at each sentence and ask yourself: "If my reader only reads this one sentence, and not one more word in my letter, will she get the point of my letter?"

This is not really possible with every single sentence in your letter, but it's a goal to strive for and think about.

What certainly is possible is to make sure that every word and every sentence contributes significantly to making the sale—that is, to persuading your reader to do what you want...*now*.

The editing process might take many days. You will need to put your letter aside for 24 hours, edit it, set it aside for another 24 hours, and edit it some more.

T.S. Eliot's epic poem *The Waste Land* was perhaps the greatest poem of the twentieth century only because of ruthless editing by his fellow poet Ezra Pound. Ezra Pound was not as great a poet as Eliot, but he was a great and ruthless editor. I'm sure Eliot did not like it one bit when Pound crossed out most of Eliot's first draft of *The Waste Land*. Pound threw most of Eliot's poem in the garbage. But Eliot trusted Pound's judgment. Eliot was too close to the text, which he had written, to be objective.

Cutting copy for a writer is like slashing your own flesh with a knife. I wince when I discard a sentence, or a paragraph, or a page, or sometimes an entire letter that I have worked so hard to write. When I cut my own copy, I feel like I am losing part of myself...forever.

But Ezra Pound was determined to force Elliot to cut every extra word, to boil the poem down to its purest essence. Through ruthless and painful editing, Ezra Pound helped Eliot create one of the great works of western literature. Without Pound's ruthless, almost sadistic editing, no one would have paid much attention to *The Waste Land* by T.S. Eliot.

Eliot's poem was a classic because every word counted. Before Pound's editing, Eliot's poem was nice—like a glass of milk. Nothing wrong with it. But after Pound got through with the editing, every word was like acid—highly concentrated, potent, powerful. "April is the cruelest month," the poem begins.

Editing is as painful a process as writing, actually far more painful because writing is often self-indulgence, whereas editing is more like surgery. But this surgery is absolutely essential to making your marketing letters highly concentrated and potent...like acid.

Chapter Fifty-One
The reply envelope

Spend time on the reply envelope.

Put text on reply envelopes reminding the reader what steps you want taken and to draw attention to the reply envelope.

Never pass up an opportunity to restate the offer and the need for an immediate reply. The reply envelope is a great place to remind your customer that calling the toll-free 1.800 number or ordering online will allow for more rapid delivery of the product.

Remind the reader what else to include in the reply envelope in addition to a check. Make the reply envelope as big as possible. People don't put large checks in tiny reply envelopes.

I sometimes like to fold the reply envelope to draw attention to it. Sometimes I put graphics on the reply envelope to approximate the look of a USPS PRIORITY MAIL envelope or FedEx envelope. If I'm selling a high-ticket item, I'll include a real USPS Priority Mail reply envelope. Or I'll affix first-class postage stamps to the reply envelope to emphasize the need for a reply.

If you decide to spend the money to affix first-class postage to the reply envelope, be sure to use at least three stamps that add up to the first-class postage rate, never just one stamp. I like to use as many as eight stamps on the reply envelope to draw the reader's attention to the reply envelope.

Most direct mail packages I see miss an opportunity to use the reply envelope to underscore the need for a rapid response. An impressive reply envelope will make your business and offer look more serious. I believe focusing special attention on the reply envelope can boost response 20 percent.

Chapter Fifty-Two
Make the case for why your reader must answer your letter right now

Urgency is a must in every direct marketing letter.

Your letter should have a deadline for response and should explain what dire consequence will happen if the order or reply does not arrive by the deadline. Dire might be too strong a word. We must always avoid hype, or your claimed urgency will lose credibility.

But you never want your readers to feel they can put your letter aside, go onto something else, and come back to it later. You don't want your reader to think, "It does not appear essential for me to deal with this now, maybe I'll get to it later, perhaps sometime next week."

Here's the basic idea, taken from a letter I wrote:

```
Although the absolute and final
registration deadline is _____, please
keep in mind that once all spaces are
filled, the seminar will be closed. This
seminar always fills up long before the
registration deadline.

To avoid being left out, I strongly
encourage you to call 1.800_____ today
to secure your reservation immediately.
```

You will come up with your own reasons tailored to the facts of your offer and your particular situation.

You want your readers to feel they must act before they put your letter aside, because once they put your letter down, the odds they'll ever come back to it are cut drastically.

A reader putting your letter down is just like a potential car buyer leaving a car dealership. Once the customer tells the salesman, "I'll think about what you've told me and maybe come back later," the odds of this customer ever coming back to buy a car from this salesman are very low.

Urgency is not created by using a lot of frantic sounding language.

Many writers think they are creating a sense of urgency by using the word "urgent" a lot, or other empty words like emergency, critical, and vital. It's not that you should never use these words in your letters. But these words are grossly overused by most direct mail copywriters.

You'll be far more persuasive if you just give good solid reasons for why a reply is needed today, right now, not next week or next month.

Chapter Fifty-Three
Repeat, repeat, repeat

Repeat, repeat, repeat your message is a key marketing principle.

Nike, McDonald's, Crest, Tide, and the most successful consumer brands show the same ads over and over again because they know it will take many impressions on your brain before their message sinks in. The same is true in direct mail, which is just another form of advertising.

Your message must be simple, focused, and repeated over and over again to your target market. Just because they answered your letter once does not mean they remember answering it. Nor does it mean they could explain to their friends what your business actually does. Most people buy in response to a direct mail letter out of impulse.

They liked what they read at that moment, bought your product, and then went on to something else. A few days later, they've forgotten your letter completely.

The big advertisers know this fact of life.

They know they can't stop repeating their message to their target audience. They know the battle for market share is really a battle for a share of people's attention, a battle for minds.

That's why you should continue mailing a successful prospect package until it stops working. It's also why you should not "undupe" your customer list against prospect lists, except for the best 20 percent or 30 percent of your customers or clients...who clearly do know about what you do and should be treated as the great friends to you that they are.

More on this last point later.

Chapter Fifty-Four
The most powerful sentence construction in sales

Which of these two headlines do you think will sell more?

"Lose 10 pounds in 10 days"

Or...

"If you will give me 30 minutes of your time, I will show you how to lose 10 pounds in 10 days."

Both headlines are sound fundamentally. They are claims of fact and do not include any empty hype words such as "incredible" or "amazing."

You might choose the first sentence because it's short and direct. The reader knows in two seconds what this product is about.

So that's a true strength of the first sentence.

But the second, much longer sentence was far more successful—generating 53% more inquiries to be exact.

Here's why.

People are bombarded with advertising pitches all day long. Their mailboxes and email boxes are packed with junk mail and spam. People's minds are conditioned to be skeptical of every claim they hear. It's now automatic reflex to tune out claims, because most claims are false. Most claims are not believable.

So, in a desperate attempt to improve response, most direct marketers and sales letter writers will increase their claims to preposterous levels, in the hope that they will get a few suckers to bite.

By taking this approach, most advertisers remove the most important prerequisite for having any chance of closing a sale—credibility.

As soon as your reader or listener hears a single claim that sounds false, or that sounds like all the usual advertising hype they see everyday all day long, they tune out.

The longer headline is believable. It's believable because the proposition requires something of the reader. The first headline requires nothing of the reader. The first headline implies that no work will be required of the reader to lose the weight—no sacrifice, no pain. The first headline sounds like all the other weight-loss claims that you hear everyday.

The second headline makes it clear up front that the reader will need to spend 30 minutes on this project this week if she wants to lose the 10 pounds.

The fact that something is required of the reader is attention-getting in itself.

When was the last time you heard an ad for a diet or weight-loss program that suggested work or sacrifice might be required to lose the weight?

Most people understand that nothing is really free in this life, and that true gain will certainly require some pain. A *quid pro quo* proposition is far more persuasive than a claim that suggests something is free, or effortless, or requires nothing in return. *Surely, something unpleasant will be required for me to lose 10 pounds in 10 days* will be the thought that runs through any intelligent person's mind.

Conventional wisdom in marketing is that "free" is the most powerful word in advertising.

Maybe that was the case 100 years ago, but not so anymore.

I believe the most powerful word in advertising is "IF."

More precisely, the most persuasive sentence construction in advertising is the **"IF...THEN"** proposition. "If you will do X, I will help you do Y."

It's the *quid pro quo* proposition. That makes sense to people. We say right up front that something will be required of the reader—in this case, most likely, it will be some hard work and perhaps cutting down on desserts if there really is a chance to lose 10 pounds in 10 days.

Starting with an "If you will do X, I will do Y" proposition immediately diffuses a reader's skepticism. The mere word "IF" signals to the reader, even if only subconsciously, that the writer might not be blowing smoke. People love to hear propositions and proposals.

Some of my very best marketing letters start with the sentence: "I have a proposal for you."

The next sentence will then start with "IF..."

"If you will do X, then Y" will happen. Or "If you will do X, I will do Y."

The word "IF" triggers the mind to start paying attention. The word "IF" signals to listeners that the speaker or writer is about to say something that makes sense, something that sounds a little like a mathematical equation: "IF X...then Y."

It sounds like iron-clad logic.

By contrast, starting your conversation by making some fantastic claim that seems to defy common sense, and which is unsupported by any facts or anything in your reader's experience, and to suggest this fantastic benefit is free and requires no sacrifice, may be the fastest way to destroy your credibility and ensure your letter is pitched in the trash.

I once had a salesman come into my office and ask me, "Would you like to have an extra million dollars this year?"

I answered "Of course. And I also wish rain water were beer. Please leave my office."

The **"IF...THEN"** proposition lays the first brick on the road to persuading your prospect to start listening to you. That first all-important brick is to establish credibility, to say very clearly that you are requiring something of your reader.

Chapter Fifty-Five
The single most persuasive word

Again, **contrary to conventional** advertising wisdom, the most persuasive words in selling are not "free" and "new."

The word "BECAUSE" is far more persuasive.

Why?

BECAUSE this word signals to the reader that you have reasons for making the claims you are asserting...

BECAUSE this word instantly lets your reader know that you have facts to back up what you say...

BECAUSE this word shows your reader that you have put thought into your letter.

Similar to the "If X...then Y" sentence construction I described in the previous section, BECAUSE is a great word for building credibility. The word BECAUSE signals that you have facts to support what you are saying. "Hire me BECAUSE..." is so much stronger than just leaving it as "HIRE ME!"

And adding an exclamation mark does not strengthen the argument one bit.

Facts sell. And reasons sell...BECAUSE facts and reasons persuade. The word "BECAUSE" tells your reader that the rest of the sentence will be "a reason why" what you claim is true, or a reason why I am asking you to take some action.

Suppose your 10-year-old child made this request: "Mom, can I come home later tonight and miss dinner?"

Your response would **not** be, "Sure, no problem. Come home whenever you can." It would be to say, "No, absolutely not. Get home right now and start your homework." Or you might come back with a very skeptical, "Why?"—knowing your answer will still be "No."

Your child will have a far greater chance of getting an immediate "yes" if he asked the same question this way: "Mom, can I come home after dinner tonight BECAUSE I've already finished my homework and BECAUSE Jimmy's mom has invited me to have dinner there with them."

The word BECAUSE is very disarming BECAUSE this word tells you that your child is about to follow his seemingly out-of-the-ordinary request with a set of reasons and facts that can easily be checked out. You might still answer "No" after hearing his reasons and facts. You might indeed have a stronger set of facts and reasons for denying his request. But the conversation is now engaged. And your son has a far greater chance of getting a "yes" answer from you...all BECAUSE he immediately followed his request with the word "BECAUSE."

Chapter Fifty-Six
The #1 mistake made by writers of sales letters

Facts, **reasons, logical arguments**, fascinating details, and a great story all help you sell.

The fastest way to guarantee your letter is thrown in the trash is to use the typical empty hype-words amateur writers use all the time in their sales letters.

You know these words well—words like "amazing," "incredible," "awesome," the "best ever," "colossal," and the "greatest."

With compelling facts, reasons, and a good story to tell, there's no reason to use these kinds of meaningless hype words. But these hype words are used so often that not only are they not attention-getting in the least, they have actually become trigger words that cause a reflex action in readers to stop reading immediately.

Most amateur sales letter writers think raising the volume and screaming at the reader is the best way to make sure the reader is listening—when actually it's the surest way to cause your prospect to tune out.

Good copywriting does not imitate the approach of street corner huckster.

The best salesmen are those who have a knack for selling without customers even realizing they are being sold to. The instant your prospect sees that she is being sold something, the truth detector machinery in the brain goes on full alert and your reader becomes a super skeptic.

Who are you more likely to hire to do a job?

The fellow who is trying to sell you hard, the fellow who seems desperate for work? Or the fellow who does not need the job because he has plenty of business already, the fellow who must clear a spot in his schedule for you because his services are in such demand?

When Stephen King writes, does he use a lot of hype to generate reader interest? Does he scream at the reader? Does he say, "Okay reader, now get ready for the scary part, because this is going to be really, really scary"?

No, he simply tells the story. Readers are pulled along by the fascinating details, the mystery, the intrigue, the suspense, and the story line. This is how Stephen King gets people to stay up all night reading one of his 600-page books.

Great writers know how to hold the attention of readers without the empty hype. Study Stephen King and how he holds your attention. You will then write much better letters.

Remember, Stephen King is a salesman too. He sells books for a living, and he's sold a lot of them. But it does not matter one bit to his customers that Stephen King is selling them books, because we are completely immersed in the story he's telling and the fascinating details. We want him to keep writing books...so we can buy more.

Chapter Fifty-Seven
The most important rule in sales

Obviously, we need to be completely honest and candid in all our business and financial dealings simply as a moral imperative, even if honesty did not work. That should go without saying.

But that's not why I'm saying "scrupulous honesty is the most important rule in all sales."

The great news for marketers is that honesty is one of the most powerful and effective sales tools.

The reason is the American people have become experts at immediately detecting scams and false claims because they have now seen so many. An exaggeration, a claim that seems the least bit suspect, will cause your readers to dismiss everything else you have to say. In fact, they will just stop reading as soon as they sense they are the target of a snow job.

That's why in all my sales letters I make sure to clearly state— even highlight—my weaknesses and shortcomings right up front.

Why do I do this?

Well, for one thing it's probably readily apparent to anyone who meets me what my strengths and weaknesses are. It would be a completely futile exercise to try to present myself as something different than what I am.

Another reason to admit your weaknesses up front in any sales presentation is that it establishes your credibility. It's disarming. You will immediately see your listeners' guard come down.

And then I will turn my readily admitted weaknesses into strengths.

For example, I usually tell audiences of aspiring entrepreneurs that "I can't hold down an office job in a big company for long, which is why I had no choice but to go into business for myself."

Who would ever admit such a thing?

The audience's ears immediately perk up. They want to hear more. After that shocking admission, I then say something like:

> The truth is, most successful entrepreneurs would be fired instantly from most jobs at big established companies...because they like doing things their own way. They don't have much patience for bureaucracy and meetings. They have no time for office politics. They are men and women of action. They don't wait for orders from headquarters. They hear the gunfire and ride to the sound of the guns. They don't wait for the committee to decide what needs to be done. When the entrepreneur sees a problem, he tackles it, instantly.
>
> The entrepreneur is not worried about covering his rear end. He just wants to get the job done, and done now. Unfortunately, this is not a personality that is appreciated in most large corporate bureaucracies. Corporate bureaucracies can't act quickly, which is why they always hire consultants like me to do what needs to be done... because I can be easily fired. And I don't mind one bit. As a consultant, especially as a marketing consultant, my entire job is to

```
solve a marketing problem and then get fired
and move on to solve someone else's
marketing problem.
```

Admitting your weakness up front makes everything else you have to say more believable. Admitting your weaknesses and shortcomings also helps define who you are and what you do, why you are different from your competitors...who will never admit their weaknesses.

```
We're not big, established, famous, or
prestigious. But because we're small and
new, we're more flexible. We'll work harder
for your business. Your hard-earned dollar
will go a lot farther with us. We'll care
more about you; and your account won't be
handled by an inexperienced junior account
manager. You'll be dealing everyday with the
head of this company, who has more than 20
years experience in this industry.
```

Avis deployed this ad strategy brilliantly against Hertz, which is the bigger car rental company. Avis admitted in its ad campaign: "We're #2, so we'll try harder."

What an endearing ad campaign. Plus, Americans love an underdog. Avis is not likely ever to pass Hertz as the biggest car rental company. But being #2 isn't bad. Most of us would take it.

So, not only is honesty a moral imperative, it's an extremely effective sales strategy.

Think of this truth this way:

Your customers, your clients are not idiots. They are very intelligent people who hear sales pitches all the time. They know when they are being conned. When a salesman walks into their office or when a direct mail pitch arrives in the mail, their immediate reaction is to get rid of the salesman as quickly as possible and to pitch the direct mail piece in the trash. That's always your potential customer's first impulse.

But obvious honesty and candor where you admit weakness instantly diffuses skepticism. The skeptic's antennae start to go down. Your prospective customer starts to like you and believe what you have to say—that is, until you make a claim that appears to be hype.

Chapter Fifty-Eight
The #1 way to make sure you succeed in marketing and in business

Focus on helping other people achieve success.

The only way to persuade someone to buy is to offer what he needs or what she is looking for. It's not about what you want. Success in business and in sales lies in figuring out what others want and how to solve other people's problems.

One reason I love marketing, sales, and business is that I am always forced to walk in the shoes of others—to put myself in their place when crafting my sales letters and presentations.

I must figure out, "What can I do to solve their problem? How can I help them? How can I be of true service? How can I be a godsend to them?"

Businesses fail because they focus on their own needs, their own goals, their own wants, their own timetables...instead of on what their customer wants.

So be a problem solver. More on point, be a solver of other people's problems.

If you focus on helping others, most of your problems will fix themselves along the way.

Forgetting this seemingly obvious principle is the #1 reason for failure in marketing and in business.

Chapter Fifty-Nine
Raise the level of your guarantee

It's no longer sufficient simply to include a money-back guarantee with your offers. There is nothing remarkable about a money-back guarantee, since all marketers include it.

Snoresville.

The challenge is showing your reader that your guarantee means something, that it's real. This reminds me of the Chris Farley line from the movie "Tommy Boy": "Look, if you want me to take a dump in a box and mark it 'Guaranteed,' I will."

That's about how much credence your readers place in the word "guaranteed" today.

How do you make your guarantee mean something? How do you make your readers pay attention to your guarantee?

What's required today is a super-charged guarantee—a guarantee, frankly, that requires brass balls (if you're a guy).

Nordstrom's guarantee is one of the most famous.

Nordstrom promises that you can return a Nordstrom product anytime and get a full refund, no matter how long you've had it, no matter how much you've worn it.

There's a story (probably an urban legend) about a guy who brought in a set of tires to Nordstrom, asking for a refund. Nordstrom gave the refund even though Nordstrom has never sold tires. Even though this story is probably myth, the fact that the story is out there just underscores the legendary fame the Nordstrom guarantee has achieved.

Everyone knows about the Nordstrom eye-popping guarantee. The Nordstrom guarantee is so famous that it's now part of the Nordstrom brand. This extraordinary guarantee is what people think of when they think of Nordstrom.

The Nordstrom guarantee communicates far more than just the purchase is "risk-free" to the customer. This super-charged guarantee communicates that Nordstrom has confidence in the quality of its merchandise, and also that Nordstrom trusts its customers to treat Nordstrom fairly. A relationship of trust is established.

Nordstrom is telling customers that the store is staking its entire business on the quality of its products and on customer satisfaction. In a sense, Nordstrom has built its business and reputation on the attention-getting strength of its guarantee.

And what a brilliant marketing strategy this is, because without this memorable guarantee, Nordstrom would not stand out in people's minds as any different from Nieman Marcus, Bloomingdale's, Macy's, Fields, Saks Fifth Avenue, or a dozen other department stores that offer the very same merchandise. The stunning Nordstrom guarantee is what makes Nordstrom different.

I know an accountant who promises his customers that if they ever feel he has failed to save them at least double the cost of his fee on their income taxes versus what they would have paid if they had done their own taxes, he will refund his entire fee.

This accountant has no shortage of clients. As far as I know, he has never been asked for a refund.

One of the biggest challenges we sales letter writers have is to get our readers to read our entire letter—to hear the entire pitch. One way to generate interest in your letter is to build your letter around a stunning guarantee that might read like this:

<u>This Letter Is Guaranteed</u>

You might wonder: "How can a letter be guaranteed?" It's free anyway!

I don't believe this guarantee has ever been made before. So here's how it works:

If you read my entire letter and if you feel, at the end, that it's been a waste of your time, just let me know by writing a note on the back of this certificate and I will send you $20, or donate $40 to the Salvation Army, whichever you prefer.

I am making this guarantee because I know you are very busy running your dry cleaning business. I also know that I am asking you to take a few minutes of your valuable time to consider how the program

I've outlined here can help improve your
marketing of your dry cleaning business.

I used to worry about making such a
guarantee. Since I'm sending out about
400 of these invitations, this means I
might conceivably need to pay out as much
as $16,000. But I'm not worried any more
because I know most entrepreneurs, like
you, have integrity. And I know that
almost every entrepreneur and small
business owner sees a need to improve
their marketing.

Sincerely,

Ben Hart

Sure, there will be a few jokers out there who will request the $20. But most people (98% or more) truly are people of honor and integrity. Nordstrom would have gone out of business long ago if the average consumer had any interest in cheating the store.

Contrary to the impression we might have from the nightly newscasts, the wonderful truth is that the vast majority of people are decent, honest, hardworking folks who won't take advantage of you and won't try to cash in on your super-charged guarantee.

Chapter Sixty
Turn manure into fertilizer

To survive in business, especially when you are small and just starting, you must be creative. You must always ask yourself, how can I turn my obvious weakness into a marketing advantage?

And sometimes your weakness can become a true advantage.

I touched on this earlier. I'll show you what I mean.

You're a farmer. You have a big pile of horse manure sitting in your yard. Is this manure? Or is this fertilizer? You can make a whole lot more money selling fertilizer than you can selling manure.

Most people don't have much use for lemons. You might need a little lemon juice once in a while for your fish. But that's about it. Lemons are sour and bitter. No one likes lemon juice, at least not by itself. Lemons are considered undesirable items, which is why we call new cars that don't work "lemons."

But add some sugar to the lemon juice, and you have lemonade. You can sell gallons of lemonade to people, especially to kids, in the summer.

In all your marketing efforts, constantly think of ways you can turn your lemons into lemonade and your manure into fertilizer. Admit your weaknesses (your lemons) and turn your weaknesses into strengths (lemonade).

Some of America's richest people got rich by selling dirt, gravel, saw dust, wood shavings, even garbage. Your used paper that's just gone through the shredder is not shredded paper, it's confetti.

I know a woman who makes a fortune going to yard sales and buying junk for almost nothing and reselling the junk as antiques.

Your weakness is that you are just one guy starting your business and you have no money. Your competitors are big operations with lots of employees, horsepower, and money, and everyone knows who they are. But now assess your strengths.

You don't have the overhead. You have fewer personnel problems. You are flexible and can adjust quickly. I know lots of heads of big successful companies who wish they could go back to just being one guy again starting a business. They were freer back then. They could get things done. They were not held hostage by their own bureaucracy. Would your clients like to deal with the #1 guy at the company, or a wet-behind-the-ears, 24-year-old, junior account executive in a big corporate bureaucracy who has no experience and frankly does not care much about the client or even the company he works for? Many people want to deal with the #1 guy in the small start-up company, the guy who actually cares, not a functionary. Turn this into a marketing advantage.

Spare me from negative, lazy people. They will always bring you down. Avoid them like the plague. Be positive and creative. As in jujitsu, use your competitor's weight and momentum against him. Turn your weakness into strength. Never look at your weakness as weakness. With a little imagination, thought and creativity, you can turn the tables on and out-maneuver your bigger and richer, but also fatter and lazier competition.

Adopt this mindset, and most of your business problems will be solved.

Chapter Sixty-One
The purpose of graphic art

Graphic art and appearance is crucial to the success of a direct mail package, but not to make the package look pretty. The purpose of graphic art is to allow you to instantly communicate your message to your reader. You do this principally with headlines.

The purpose of a headline is to reach out and grab the reader—to tell the reader what your letter is about, to create enough intrigue and interest for your reader to want to keep reading.

So often I've seen graphic art actually obscure the message of a direct mail piece. Graphics should enable your reader to grasp the message of your package in three seconds or less. Simple layouts are best. Not only are simple layouts far less costly to produce, but simple is far more effective.

In direct mail marketing it's plain Jane, not the prettiest girl at the party, who wins.

Words, not graphics, not even pictures, are the most powerful way to communicate ideas. If you use photos, they are to reinforce your words. Photos may or may not be useful in your sales piece, and can help you get the attention of your reader. But it's the copy that does the selling. You can sell without pictures; you can't sell without words.

The Bible has no pictures, only words, and it's the best selling book of all time. Of course you want your packages to look good and professional. But the purpose of graphics is to grab the reader's attention and help your reader know instantly what you are saying.

Also, a big part of what makes direct mail successful is that the letter must look and feel like a communication from one person to another. Your letter and package really should not look like it's from a large impersonal corporation. You don't receive letters from corporations. You receive letters from individuals. Let's hope no one is receiving letters signed by Exxon.

Chapter Sixty-Two

How to get
your envelope opened

You can write the greatest sales letter in the world, but if no one notices your letter in the mailbox, if it just looks like all the other junk mail, your pitch is doomed.

Big consumer product companies know this, which is why they spend so much money, time, effort, and research on packaging. They want their product to stand out on the shelf in a supermarket.

You want your letter to stand out in the mailbox.

I pay a lot of attention to the outer envelope or carrier, also called the wrapper, on self-mailers. Getting the recipient of your letter to open your envelope is the first battle you must win with your reader.

When people sort their mail, they generally put them in three piles: personal letters from friends and relatives; bills they must pay by a certain date; and commercial junk mail.

Most commercial junk mail will go in the trash. A few pieces of bulk rate mail will be kept if they look intriguing.

Since everyone reads personal letters from friends and relatives that arrive with first-class postage, your best strategy is to send your letter with first-class postage stamps and make your envelope look like it contains a personal letter from a friend. These letters should arrive in a non-window closed-face envelope. A handwritten address on the carrier can be very effective for the right offer. Everyone who receives such an envelope will open it.

But if the item you are selling is inexpensive and the profit margin small, the problem with sending a first-class letter can be cost. If your profit on the item you are selling is only $15 or $25, and if you are expecting a response rate of 2-3%, you will likely need to mail at the bulk rate. You'll need to do a little math to determine whether you should mail first class or at the bulk rate.

When you're sending bulk rate mail, you must come up with other ways to entice people to open your envelope. Usually the best way is to create a sense of mystery and intrigue.

Sometimes the most effective strategy is with no copy or teaser at all. Just a blank envelope, not even a return address. Another strategy is to make your envelope look like an important government document, as if it might be from the IRS or the Department of Motor Vehicles. "Monitored Delivery" is a phrase I sometimes use on my outer envelopes. "Financial Documents Enclosed" is another phrase I sometimes use if the package contains a prospectus. "Final Notice" is a teaser I sometimes use if I've written a prospect several times with the same offer, but have yet to receive a response.

As a general rule, headline-style teaser copy broadcasting what's inside the envelope is hazardous. Extensive testing shows most teasers depress response. One reason is that headline-style advertising copy on outer envelopes telegraphs to the reader that this is advertising mail, that it's junk mail. But a really good teaser can sometimes outperform a mysterious carrier.

A teaser I used stated in big bold red type:

"At last...a Christian Alternative to AARP!"

This worked better than all other outer envelope approaches I tried with this particular prospecting appeal. Why? Because there were millions of Christians out there who were interested in a Christian Alternative to AARP. Enough senior citizens were peeved enough with AARP's consistently liberal lobbying activities that this opened up a market for a conservative Christian alternative. I mailed millions of copies of this letter for the Christian Seniors Association.

But even here, the mystery carriers worked almost as well. Using a headline on the outer envelope to grab interest is a risky proposition.

When in doubt, I'll use the far safer strategy of creating a sense of mystery.

In most cases, I don't like to put the name of the organization on the outer envelope, even for offers to my most loyal customers. Not only does putting the name of the organization on the carrier envelope advertise that this is probably a sales pitch, it also tells the reader that this is not a personal letter from a friend. It screams that this is an institutional mailing, which automatically places the letter in a second, third, or even lower category of importance.

Think of the psychology of envelope opening this way. Is a child more excited at Christmas to see a pile of presents wrapped in colored paper hiding what's inside all those boxes? Or would the child prefer to arrive at the tree on Christmas morning and see all her presents in plain view with no pretty wrapping paper? It's far more exciting to have no idea what's in all those boxes. Children are delirious with delight as they frantically rip off all that wrapping paper to find out what's hiding inside.

I think the same psychology is at work in designing outer envelopes for your direct mail offers. More often than not, you will do better by creating a sense of mystery and intrigue with your envelopes—but not always. There's also a lot to be said for that one unwrapped present standing under the Christmas tree if it's an especially wonderful present, a present that will create excitement by itself, even though not wrapped—perhaps a shiny red bicycle.

I agonize for hours, sometimes days, over what to put on my outer envelope. Is the offer compelling and exciting enough to broadcast what's inside with a headline-style teaser? Or should I stick with the far safer mystery strategy? Ninety percent of the time I will opt for creating mystery with my outer envelopes.

However, you probably should not use the mystery strategy if you're fortunate enough to have your letter signed by a celebrity or famous person. In that case, you might want to advertise that the envelope contains a letter from a celebrity. Do this by putting the famous person's name in the upper left corner of the carrier. Make the envelope look like it contains a personal letter from the famous person. The outer envelope should be designed to look like it's the famous person's personal stationery.

More thoughts on packaging

Sometimes standard #10 envelopes and smaller carriers are not big enough for all the materials you want to send to your prospect or customer.

If I have a lot of material I want to send, I'll often put it in a 9"x

12" Tyvek envelope—the kind you'll see in an office supply store. Tyvek is that tough fibrous material that you can't tear. It comes with a green "First Class" headline on the front and a green half-diamond pattern around the border. It also comes in plain white if you want to mail at the bulk mail rate to save on postage. You can't write or print on Tyvek easily because it's so slippery and fibrous, so you will need a label to address your package.

The Tyvek carrier is very attention-getting. It signals that something very important must be inside. And the weight of the material inside is also attention-getting and provokes curiosity. Everyone will open a large Tyvek envelope—unless you telegraph what's inside. Don't put the name of your organization anywhere on the outside. Do not signal in anyway that this is advertising mail or a sales pitch. Its power is in both the mystery of what's inside and also in that it certainly looks like it must be a personal communication—a serious letter with important material inside.

I'm a big fan of the Tyvek carrier and I use it often. The downside is that it's expensive compared to paper envelopes. So you can only use this carrier if you are selling a higher-priced item. It's great for business-to-business offers because it looks like a serious business communication. And it will likely get through the secretary and to the decision-maker.

I also often send marketing letters and offers in boxes. Everyone will open a box. But you will need something besides paper to put in a box—such as a video or perhaps a gift. Everyone is excited when the UPS man delivers a mysterious box. So, again I repeat, do not hint with headline copy or other graphics on your box mailing that this is a sales offer.

If you are inviting someone to a seminar, a conference, a grand opening, or a fundraising event, packaging the offer in a wedding-style invitation with calligraphy addressing can be very effective. Everyone will open a wedding invitation or an invitation that looks like it's for an exclusive, prestigious event. I always include a letter along with the impressive wedding-style invitation that explains the event the prospect is being invited to.

I have also sent offers in clear plastic carriers if what's inside looks valuable or interesting, or pitch-black plastic bags if I want the mailing to look ominous and mysterious. I have mailed offers in bubble packs, tubes, and even between two pieces of cardboard stapled together. Everyone will open that just out of curiosity. I typically deploy super-creative and unusual packaging when I must mail at the bulk rate, rather than first class, to save on postage. So I must come up with unusual packaging that will get attention, provoke interest, and draw attention from the fact that this is bulk-rate mail—that it's junk mail.

If I am mailing my offer at the first-class rate, I will want to telegraph to the reader that this is first-class mail, not junk mail. I do this by putting at least three stamps that add up to the first-class postage amount on the carrier envelope. The more stamps the better. Using lots of stamps on your carrier also gives your letter a more personal look and feel.

Some mailshops are able to produce blue handwritten fonts that look like real handwriting. You have to examine the printing very closely to see that it was produced by an ink jet. A hand-addressed carrier, or one that looks hand-addressed, is far more likely to be opened than a carrier that has clearly been addressed by a machine. If at all possible, always avoid using the old Cheshire labels that advertise that this is junk mail going to many others.

Obviously these rules do not apply for certain kinds of commercial offers, such as the coupon and card packs we all get in the mail addressed to the "Resident." But these don't contain letters. The purpose of the letter is to communicate to your prospect that this is a personal communication from one person to another. When writing a sales letter—whether the target is a consumer or a high-level business executive—your aim in your packaging, as much as cost and your budget allows, is to convey the impression that this is a personal letter.

It's very important to make every effort to change the look of your packages. Try not to fall into a rut of making everything look the same. With your graphic art, use different borders and layouts while being careful not to allow the graphic art to overwhelm the headlines. Visit letter shops to find out what others are mailing. New formats and technologies are coming out all the time. Meet with printers and envelope manufacturers to find out what's available to vary the look and feel of your packages and increase the impact of your packages.

How much should you spend on personalization and packaging?

This depends on a number of factors, the two most important being: How many orders will be generated by the additional investment; and what is the profit on each order?

If your profit is less than $50 and your anticipated response rate is 2%, you cannot spend nearly as much as you can if your anticipated response rate is 2%, but your profit per-sale is $100 or $1,000 or more.

Increasing the level of your personalization will, in almost every case, increase the odds of your letter being read and will increase your response rate. The question is: Is the added cost worth the increased response rate? What is your return on investment?

Magazine subscription offers are usually non-personalized "Dear Friend"-type letters because magazine subscriptions are relatively low-cost and have a narrow profit margin. In this case, adding another nickel or dime to the cost of your package is a major consideration.

But if what you are selling is membership in an exclusive club of business leaders, and if the membership dues are $1,500 or $5,000 a year, the invitation offer would have to be impressive.

Such a mailing should be an impressive, highly-personalized, high-impact invitation, not only because that's what would be expected, but also because the profit margin is so much greater. Where you might only be able to spend 40 or 50 cents per letter to send a magazine subscription offer, you might be able to spend $4 on an invitation to join an exclusive club where the annual membership dues are $1,500 or $5,000.

Again, it's just a mathematical calculation. The figures you need to do the math are: 1) your profit margin on the product you're selling; 2) your expected rate of return on the mailings; and 3) how much the additional investment in personalization and more impressive packaging will increase your rate of response.

The only way you can know the answers to the second and third questions is by testing.

Chapter Sixty-Three
The most important word in direct marketing

The word is "TEST."

Direct marketing is not about conjecture.

Nor is it about being creative, original, or finding new frontiers and "going where no man has gone before."

Direct mail marketing is a science developed largely through trial and error. We know what we know mostly because of our past successes and failures. And much of what has proven true in direct marketing we could not have guessed.

Who would have thought long letters would work better than short letters most of the time?

We know because of the results of head-to-head tests. We also know that long letters do not work best all the time.

How do we know? Because of test results.

We know surveys can work, sweepstakes contests can work, and that membership offers can work (depending on the situation)...all because of tests.

How can we know how much to charge for our product until we test different prices? How can we possibly know what combination of incentives in our offer will produce the most orders without test results?

Will our prospect respond better to free frequent flier miles for using our credit card, or "cash back rewards"?

We can't know without test results.

We can make educated guesses. We can have theories. But there's only one way we know if our guesses are right or wrong: TEST.

Without test results, without data, we are flying blind.

Testing will humble even the most expert direct marketers.

Usually a large 9" x 12" carrier will generate more orders than a smaller standard #10, but not always. Usually a personalized letter will produce a bigger response than an off-set non-personalized "Dear Friend" letter, but not always.

Contrary to what you might have guessed, including a pretty, four-color glossy brochure with your letter will usually depress your returns, but not always.

Sometimes postage-paid Business Reply Envelopes (BREs) work better than reply envelopes that require readers to affix their own stamp, but certainly not always.

In a recent mailing, I was sure putting stamps on the reply envelope would be far more impressive and produce bigger returns than a less personal-looking commercial standard Business Reply Envelope (BRE) you see in junk mail everyday.

A head-to-head test proved otherwise. But this could, and likely will, change for another mailing and another offer to different lists.

Test different headlines. Test formats. Test mailing first class versus mailing at the bulk rate. Test a variety of offers and combinations of offers. Test colors and fonts. Test arguments and reasons.

The most important tests are tests of lists and list segments.

With every mailing you conduct, you should take the opportunity to test something. You only need about 50 replies for a test to be statistically valid. So if you expect a response rate of 2%, this would require mailing a test sample of 2,500 names. The larger the test sample, the more statistical validity it has. But even small tests will usually give you the answer to your question.

After more than 19 years in this business I continue to be surprised by the results of tests.

Never assume anything.

When you think about it, there really is no excuse to have a financial disaster in direct mail marketing, because you would never invest in a large mailing until you have test results.

If TEST is the most important word in direct marketing, "ASSUME" is the most dangerous word.

ASSUME is a word that leads to financial ruin.

Chapter Sixty-Four
You will never stand alone if you stand for something

When I was an undergraduate at Dartmouth College, I was one of the very few conservatives on campus.

I knew of maybe five or six other students who were also conservatives. We got together and started a renegade conservative student newspaper called the *Dartmouth Review*. Many of the articles were humor and satire, with a right-wing edge. Part of the role of the paper was to explode the notion that conservatives were humorless, stodgy fuddy-duddies who did not like sex. The paper was often accused of being sophomoric, which did not hurt our feelings much because many of us were sophomores.

At any rate, the paper caused shrieks of outrage across the campus. There were protests outside the *Review* offices. The college administration tried to shut down the paper. It would not allow the paper to be distributed in student mailboxes or placed on tables in any Dartmouth facility for people to pick up (or not) as they wished. When we distributed the paper door-to-door in the dorms, we were chased by campus police. The Dartmouth faculty assembled and voted 113-5 to denounce the paper and recommend that the paper be banned from campus. Where was the ACLU? Review editors were hauled before the College disciplinary committee on absurd trumped-up charges and recommended for expulsion.

One *Review* editor was charged with having photocopied a press release that was in plain view on the bulletin board at the college news service. He then used part of it for an article he was writing for the Review. He was charged with theft. He escaped punishment after a full-day of Kafkaesque kangaroo court hearings.

Another *Review* writer was charged with being rude at the cafeteria when there were no strawberry pancakes for breakfast, though strawberry pancakes had been listed on the menu. This became known as the "strawberry pancake incident." Though Anthony had been perhaps too vociferous in his complaint to the cafeteria manager about the absence of strawberry pancakes, he did not deserve suspension. It

How To Write...

was clear to us that he, like Clarence Thomas, had been targeted especially hard by Administration authorities because he was a black conservative. Plus he was a very funny writer. And quite a few professors did not at all like his articles describing what was really going on in their classrooms. Anthony was doomed.

But a funny thing happened.

Students came out of the woodwork to join the *Review*. We soon had scores of students writing for the paper, selling advertising (for 20% commission), and helping with distributing the paper in the dorm rooms and across campus, chased every step of the way in Keystone Cops fashion by overweight huffing-and-puffing campus police.

I wrote a bestselling book about the founding of the *Dartmouth Review* titled *Poisoned Ivy*. This was the first book to point out the "political correctness" problem that infects academia. "Political correctness" is the enemy of freedom of thought and speech.

The paper was controversial. It was also an exciting place to hang out. I wrote a subscription solicitation letter to all Dartmouth alumni. The college produced a directory of all alumni, so we simply keyed the list into a computer. We knew nothing about direct mail marketing at the time, but I figured this list was valuable. I wrote a letter describing the paper and what we were trying to do. I made it very clear that this was a conservative student newspaper with an edge.

Another point I stressed was that the paper would give alumni the truth about what was really happening on campus. No longer would alumni have to rely on the official *Alumni Magazine* (written and created by Dartmouth's fundraising department) for their news about what was happening at Dartmouth.

My letter was four pages, plus there was an order form. We mailed it at bulk rate since we could not afford first-class postage. We also mailed it in stages because we could not afford to mail all alumni at once. Without knowing it, we were doing many things right.

I had written a letter because we could not afford a slick four-color brochure (I did not know then that letters are always best and that slick brochures almost always depress returns). We were also testing and then rolling out as the letter proved successful (again, having no idea that this is the correct procedure in direct mail marketing).

Not only did subscriptions pour in, we received several $1,000 donations, one $5,000 donation and even one $10,000 contribution. We soon had more money than we knew what to do with. In fact, we quickly had a yearly budget of about $200,000—not bad for a few students. The *Dartmouth Review* soon became a major student enterprise. In fact, it's still publishing today, 27 years later.

What made the *Dartmouth Review* an astonishingly successful student marketing venture was that it stood for something.

The controversy this renegade student paper generated attracted a lot of media attention. CBS's *60 Minutes* did a story on the paper, which turned out surprisingly favorably for us. The liberal *60 Minutes* producer and reporting crew clearly had in mind a hatchet job on the paper, but apparently liked the students and did not like the administration's efforts to crack down on a student journalistic project. Evidently, concerns about the First Amendment trumped the liberal ideology that reigns at *60 Minutes*.

The point is, if you stand for something, especially if it's controversial and in the minority, you will gain followers. And your followers will be committed and loyal to you. This is why Rush Limbaugh has been such a successful radio personality. The more outrageous he is, the more he is attacked, the better he does, because the more his audience likes him. Michael Savage pushes this strategy even further. Ann Coulter is making a very profitable career out of saying controversial, often outrageous, things. Her books are always bestsellers.

I'm not arguing here that you should agree with any of these people or with me on politics.

The point is, when you stand for something, and when you are attacked for your position, your friends, those who like you, those who agree with you, will rally to your side. "The enemy of enemy is my friend" is the logic here. "If the people I oppose don't like this guy, he must be doing something right," is another way to put this principle.

Being controversial and outrageous may be the easiest way there is to make a lot of money.

Howard Stern understands this as well as anyone. There are few radio personalities more successful and profitable than Howard Stern. He is attacked all the time. I don't like him much. But there he sits, laughing all the way to the bank.

Every commercial enterprise can apply this principle to improve their marketing and selling.

In all your marketing, tell your prospects why you are different, why you are not at all like your competitors. Explain why you defy "conventional wisdom"—which, by the way, is almost always wrong anyway.

Defying conventional wisdom, by definition, differentiates you from the crowd and draws attention. Defying conventional wisdom, by definition, tells everyone you are different. You will do very well simply by doing the exact opposite of what the conventional wisdom says you should do.

Ben & Jerry's ice cream is a terrific example of how this can work for a run-of-the-mill product where there is almost infinite competition. How do you make ice cream different?

Ben & Jerry's ice cream became popular at exactly the same time we were being told everyday to get rid of all the fat in our diet—that fat was terrible for us, that fat was the lead cause of heart attacks. Ben & Jerry's made no secret of the fact that it contains more fat per scoop than any other major ice cream brand.

It also tastes a lot better because it's so thick and creamy— precisely because it contains so much fat.

I'm a very health-conscious person. I'm not overweight. But I would much rather eat Ben & Jerry's than any other ice cream because it tastes so much better. Diet ice cream never made much sense to me. Nor lite beer. Diet Pizza does not make much sense to me either. Ice cream is supposed to be dessert. It's not supposed to be good for you. It's supposed to be a treat.

If you want to indulge yourself, why not indulge yourself with the best tasting stuff?

Yes, you'll have serious health problems if you eat Ben & Jerry's all the time. And you won't be doing yourself any good if you drink beer as though it were water. But you're not supposed to do that. Ben & Jerry's was successful because it made a conscious decision to make the very best tasting ice cream without concern for how many calories or how much fat is in each scoop. I'd rather have one great tasting, high-calorie Heineken than five Miller Lite's.

In marketing, narrow is the gate to paradise. The more identifiable you are, the better you will do. Never try to be all things to all people. Never worry about controversy.

In fact, controversy can be great for you, your product, and your business. Controversy will get you noticed, will attract attention. And as long as your position, your stance, has a constituency, your path to profit is a clear one. Your task then is to find your constituency. More often than not, if you are at all competent, your constituency will find you.

All you have to do is put the bait in the water.

Turns out a lot of people did not want low-fat ice cream. Turns out a lot of people do not care what the Surgeon General thinks. Turns out a lot of people just want ice cream that tastes great, no matter what the fat content. Turns out people were sick and tired of blandness and sameness in their ice cream. What they wanted was Cherry Garcia.

So be different. Never be afraid to say exactly who you are and what you stand for. Stake out your role. Never shrink from controversy, as long as it's defensible controversy. The great thing about the Conventional Wisdom almost always being wrong is that you will become automatically controversial simply by clearly stating the truth. And controversy will cause people to talk about you, and this is good for your business.

So don't worry about controversy and don't try to be all things to all people in the vain hope of gaining a greater market share. If you keep these principles in mind, you will attract loyal followers.

Chapter Sixty-Five
It's much easier to make money in a small pond than a big pond

The easiest way to make money is to have no competitor.

That's so obvious it's hardly worth stating.

The easiest way to improve your chances of having no competitor, or very few competitors, is to identify a small market niche that you can dominate. It's better to be a big fish in a small pond than a small, struggling fish in a big pond. In the big pond, you will likely be eaten alive very quickly.

In a small pond, you will live a very happy, nearly stress-free, comfortable life.

Let's look again at my very first enterprise, *The Dartmouth Review*. This small conservative renegade and independent student paper was the only source of reporting and commentary on events at Dartmouth, written and produced entirely by students.

Talk about a refined and narrow product!

So not only was *The Dartmouth Review* different, it had staked out a monopoly. The truth is, the *Review* could have raised $500,000 a year, $1,000,000 a year, or even $10,000,000 a year.

There was almost no limit to the amount of money we, as mere students, could have brought in if we had run the paper like a business instead of as a part-time hobby.

But we were just students. We did not need more than about $150,000 or $200,000 a year to publish the paper and have some money left over for parties. So we just stopped there, sending out a fundraising letter whenever we ran out of money, about four times a year.

So when you think about your product and marketing strategy, think of ways you can give your customers something they can't get anywhere else. And it's best if your market is small and highly specialized, because then the big boys are not as likely to come in and crush you.

Highly specialized information for a niche audience is always great, especially if your niche audience is relatively easy to find. The more specialized, the smaller your potential audience—but also the more committed your audience, and the more you can charge for you newsletter or magazine.

A newsletter with just one editor can do well with 1,000 or even a few hundred subscribers...if the cost of a subscription is $95 a month.

Semiconductor News would be a good candidate for such a business model, or maybe get even more specialized than that. Maybe your publication would do best by focusing on a specific kind of semiconductor. Of course, it's critically important for the information to be really good, essential insider news that semiconductor manufacturers and developers cannot get anywhere else.

The big mistake businesses make is to try to be all things to all people.

For example, the temptation for the editor and publisher of our hypothetical *Semiconductor News* will always be to expand the reach of the publication—to cover the entire high-tech industry. The assumption here is that *Semiconductor News* will reach a wider audience and gain more readers if it becomes *High-Tech News*.

But then the publication is no longer unique. The publication is no longer as valuable to anyone. Your marketing costs will skyrocket as you try to reach this wider audience, and you will have to drop your subscription price radically to have any chance to gain readers, because you will be competing with dozens of other generalist magazines covering the high-tech industry. You will have become a commodity, always competing on price.

Time magazine can never charge much for a subscription because it's a general news magazine. It wants to be all things to all people. As a result, gaining a single subscriber is a Herculean task for *Time* and enormously costly. It takes *Time* about two years on average to pay for acquiring a new subscriber—that is, for the revenue generated by the new subscriber to cover the acquisition cost of that subscriber.

Not many enterprises, especially start-up enterprises, can afford *Time*'s business model. In fact, *Time* is having difficulty affording *Time*'s business model.

Who makes more money in medicine, the general practitioner who knows something about every health problem, or the neurosurgeon?

The specialist will always earn more.

When you think about it, the path to wealth is not to become bigger, it's to become smaller. The smaller the audience and more narrow the focus, the better off most of us will be.

My brother Matt had a rock band. It was pretty good. Very good, actually. Matt is a terrific musician.

The band was getting a solid following in San Francisco. He then decided to take his band nationwide. I advised Matt not to try that. Become big in San Francisco. Maybe just become big in your neighborhood, a subset of San Francisco. If you're good, and I mean really great, you'll break out of your neighborhood when the time is right, when you have a big enough following and when you have enough cash in your pocket. He did not listen, of course. The band launched its nationwide tour, mostly doing warm-up acts for other bigger name bands. Everything that could go wrong went wrong, just like in the movie "Spinal Tap." They ran out of money. Their bus broke down. Arguments broke out. Band members quit. Soon there was no band.

The lesson here: Become big in your own neighborhood before you go nationwide. Remember, McDonald's started as just one restaurant serving one neighborhood. Find your niche, become master of your small pond. Because unless you have a billion dollar marketing budget, you will almost certainly be eaten alive in the ocean.

Chapter Sixty-Six
The #1 business blunder

I am stunned and amazed at how few businesses pay much attention at all to their existing customers—those who have actually bought something.

Some businesses don't even keep a customer list!

But it's the first sale that's the toughest. It's much easier to make a sale to someone who has bought from you before than to someone who has never bought from you and might never have heard of you. The reasons are many and should be obvious.

Your customers bought from you because they like what you are selling. They want what you are selling. They need what you are selling. Your customers would much rather continue to do business with and buy from someone they know. They would prefer not to buy from a stranger. If your product is any good, selling your customers more of what you know they like should be like shooting fish in a barrel.

For these reasons, it's far more costly to find a new customer than to keep an old one.

Your customers should be hearing from you all the time: a postal mailing once a month, an email communication a least once a week. And not every communication should be a sales pitch. Just give your customers a steady stream of valuable useful information. If you're selling tires, send your customers tips on how to stay safe on the road by rotating tires, maintaining the correct air pressure, and how to measure the tread. Send objective information on what makes a safe tire.

With your communications, your goal is to build a relationship with your customers...because when you have a trusted relationship, you have no competition. You will have customers who will faithfully buy from you.

Chapter Sixty-Seven
The fastest, easiest way to improve your profitability

You know about the "80/20 Rule." The 80/20 Rule is part of Marketing 101. The rule is this:

- 80% of sales come from 20% of customers.

- 80% of commissions are earned by 20% of salespeople.

- 80% of the wealth in America is produced by 20% of the people.

- 80% of sales are generated by 20% of the businesses.

- 80% of your income is produced by 20% of your activities.

- 80% of your revenue is generated by 20% of your clients.

- 80% of donations are made by 20% of the donors.

The reason for this is fairly obvious.

If you observe human behavior, you'll immediately notice that about 20% of the population is pulling the wagon—that is, doing about 80% of the work and generating 80% of the wealth.

Everyone else is riding the wagon, hoping someone else will pull them along.

The great majority of people don't have the guts or energy to start their own business. Most people would rather ride along on someone else's wagon, happy enough in their 9-to-5 job and collecting a regular paycheck every month, while doing as little as possible to earn it.

In the charitable arena, the rule is the same. About 20% of the population are givers. The rest of the population are takers.

Actually, the "80/20 Rule" is more like the "90/10 Rule" if we really analyze the facts carefully.

If you were to break down the population precisely, you would see that the top 10% are the true producers and givers—the true wagon-pullers. There's a middle 60% who are happy to ride in the wagon most of the time, but will help out once in a while if they are shamed into it. And then there's the bottom 30% of the population who must be dragged behind the wagon in the dirt. These are dead weights who actually hinder progress.

So now let's rename our rule of life the 30/60/10 Rule.

- 30% are dead weight you are pulling along in the dirt.

- 60% are riding in the wagon, not doing much, but not hindering your progress either.

- 10% are doing 90% of the pulling.

The #1 mistake businesses make is to focus too little attention on the 10% of customers who are providing 90% of your income—and too much attention on the rest who aren't profitable for you at all and, most likely, are costing you money.

The tendency is to take your best customers for granted. "We don't have to worry about these customers because they love us already," is the thought process at work here. We get lazy with these customers because we know these customers are profitable. We then invest enormous effort and resources to try to make our money-losing customers profitable. We continue to send these money-losers newsletters and mailings. We continue to coax, cajole, and bribe in the hope that these people will, someday, become interested in what we are doing.

We make the dead-weight money-losers the focus of our marketing.

What a catastrophic mistake this is!

Your first step toward maximizing your profitability is to immediately cut loose the 30% of the dead weight, the people (customers and employees) who are costing you money, and will never be profitable no matter what you do. Just get rid of them and at least make your wagon lighter to pull.

Your next step is to give your top 10% or 20% a lot more tender loving care and to offer more and more of whatever it is that makes these gold-plated customers love you so much. If they like milkshakes, keep offering them bigger and bigger milkshakes. Don't think *He's already had his milkshake for the month, so no need to offer another milkshake until next month.* Keep feeding your gold-plated top 10% of your customers more and more of what you know they love. And treat them as the dear and loyal friends they are to you and your business— because you can't survive and prosper without them.

Why is it that most of us are so obsessed with trying to win over the bottom 30%?

Why is it that we are more concerned with trying to turn the dead weight we're dragging along in the dirt into wagon-pullers?

I think it's because entrepreneurs are also evangelists at heart. We are so excited about whatever it is we are doing and the service we are offering that we just can't believe most people could not care less about what we are doing. We try to win them over. We are preachers who want as many people in church as we can get. We try to convert these people to the faith. We try even harder to win back our "lost sheep"—our former customers who left us. We just can't believe they left us even after all the great service we provided. It's depressing to lose a customer. Rejection is always depressing. So we spend a lot of money and effort trying to get these "lost sheep" and "prodigal children" back into the fold.

The reality is you will never turn a wagon-rider into a wagon-puller. And you will never turn dead weight even into wagon-riders, much less into wagon-pullers. We are genetically wired to be who we are. We were that way at birth.

You are far better off cutting loose the dead weight immediately. In fact, you would be better off getting rid of most of your wagon-riders. They aren't much good to you either. Keep a few of the wagon-riders around who show some potential of being wagon-pullers. And then focus 80% of your efforts on your top 20%—your very best customers and clients.

Of course, you will always need to prospect for more customers. You always need to find new prospects to pour into the top of your marketing funnel.

But you must do this knowing that only 20% (or less) of your new customers will ever be worth much to your business.

Can you see how clearly understanding this principle can affect, even dramatically change, your marketing approach? Will likely even change your business model?

With this principle in mind, your job is not to work to turn your dead weight and wagon-riders into wagon-pullers for you, but to develop a system that will identify your wagon-pullers as quickly as possible so you can focus your attention on them.

Identify, cultivate, and harvest your wheat.

Quickly identify and burn the chaff. And you will vastly increase your profitability.

Chapter Sixty-Eight
The enormous value of your "multi-buyers"

Your mailings to your customers who have bought something more than once from you will be at least three times more productive than mailings to those who have only bought something from you once.

If someone bought some exercise equipment from you, you need to be selling more exercise equipment to that person. I am amazed that so many companies only have one product to offer and have only mailed one offer to their customer list. Some businesses actually exist entirely off income from prospecting to cold lists, and have never thought of continuing to offer their list of customers more of the same. If someone buys a treadmill from you, come back with an offer for a better treadmill, or a weight machine. If a golfer buys a driver from you, offer a revolutionary new sand wedge or your new "deadeye" putter.

You know this buyer is a golfer. So keep selling him golf stuff.

A mature customer list or "housefile" is far more productive than a new housefile for the simple reason that you have identified your core of multi-buyers—your regular faithful customers.

In addition, you have stopped mailing regular offers and

promotions to most of those who have not bought anything for you in 18 or 24 months, which slashes the cost of your marketing. The older your active customer list, assuming you are mailing regularly (every month or more), the more productive it will be for each letter you mail.

For this reason, I consider the prospect program to really have two parts. There's the prospect program to your outside lists, designed to find your first-time buyers. But then there's the prospect program to your housefile that's aimed at persuading your first-time buyers to buy again. In this sense, your multi-buyers are your true housefile, because these are folks who clearly like what they are getting from you and who have made a conscious decision to continue supporting you through their purchases. They have chosen to join your family.

Chapter Sixty-Nine
What we can learn from the Grateful Dead

"The relationship between the band and the Dead Heads must be nurtured because they are us and we are them."

—Phil Lesh
Base Player with the Grateful Dead

The Grateful Dead may be the most profitable rock band in history even though it has never had a #1 single or a #1 album.

Despite the death of its leader Jerry Garcia in 1995, Grateful Dead Productions continues to generate about $60 million a year in sales and licensing fees. Pretty good for a group that no longer exists.

Jerry Garcia and the Grateful Dead were among the greatest niche marketers in history. They never pursued the top spot on the pop charts—or any ranking on the pop charts. Instead, they dedicated themselves to pursuing a distinct style of music and cultivating a face-to-face relationship with their fans, building a loyal, even fanatical community of hundreds of thousands of Dead Heads by feeding this community exactly what it wanted, never deviating from its brand, for more than 35 years.

The Grateful Dead built its following by playing an average of more than 80 concerts a year for nearly four decades. As the years and decades rolled on, the Grateful Dead's following never waned, but actually strengthened. In the early 1990s, until Garcia's death in 1995, the Grateful Dead were probably the only band that could sell out major professional football stadiums on consecutive nights with no mass-market advertising.

Except for the fact that I am a follower of the Dead, I might never have known when the Grateful Dead was coming to Washington, D.C. because they did no mass-market advertising. But every summer when the Dead came into town, the 70,000 seats at RFK stadium would be sold out for both nights instantly, as soon as the tickets went on sale.

Unlike other rock bands, the Dead would allow the Dead Heads to record their concerts and even sell the bootleg copies. In fact, a special area was set up at every concert specifically for the bootleggers, complete with sound equipment, so the recordings would be of decent quality.

Why would the band allow this?

They allowed it because a bootleg copy of a concert was free advertising for the band. The Dead believed there were no better marketers of the band than their fans. So why not let them record the concerts and distribute the tapes even if the band did not receive one cent from the sale of the tapes and CDs?

The Dead also made a decision to own every aspect of its band so it would have complete control over the production and marketing of its products. It did not want its product corrupted by traditional promoters and the big name recording labels. It put a ceiling on ticket prices, cracked down on scalpers, and did not mind at all if its hippie Dead Head fans made a few bucks by making their own Grateful Dead tie-dye shirts and products, even though not licensed by the band. It did not matter to the band that it made nothing on the "counterfeit" Grateful Dead T-shirts. The band just figured it was more free advertising.

Most importantly, the Dead made a decision to focus on its live concerts instead of recording records—because they were committed to spending face time with their fans. The Grateful Dead delivered more free concerts than any major rock band in history.

In so doing, they created a devoted community of hundreds of thousands of Dead Heads who followed them from concert to concert. You were not considered a Dead Head unless you had attended at least 100 Grateful Dead concerts.

There was also a kind of vague philosophy connecting the band and its Dead Head following. Their philosophy was intensely non-political and non-doctrinaire and went something like this: everyone should love each other or at least be nice to each other; and if more people listened to music (presumably the Dead), the world would be a much happier, less angry, more peaceful place. Kind of a naive philosophy perhaps, but it certainly worked for its fans.

Jerry Garcia and the Dead did not care one wit about being at the top of the pop music charts. They cared about staying true to their unique style of folk rock music that had a touch of bluegrass and jazz underscored by a driving beat behind every song. They cared about their fans and giving their fans one song after another that had the unmistakable Grateful Dead beat and lengthy Jerry Garcia electric guitar riffs. And they turned their fans into a community.

As a result, the other bands, even the Beatles and Rolling Stones, have pretty well faded away. Young kids today don't listen to the Beatles or the Stones much. But the Grateful Dead brand remains strong. You'll see 14-year-old kids today wearing Grateful Dead tie-dye T-shirts because they think the Dead are "cool."

Harley Davidson motorcycles also follows this basic strategy, perhaps more consciously than the Dead. Harley-Davidson motorcycles are distinctly American road machines. They are big, noisy, and ride rough. They appeal to those who have a side to them that wish they could be like "Easy Rider," those who love the freedom of the road, who like to dress in black leather, who want to look like a Hells Angel—at least for a weekend. The Harley appeals a lot to former Vietnam War veterans.

On Memorial Day Weekend, we see 250,000 Harleys roar into Washington, D.C. as part of the annual "Rolling Thunder" event, aimed at honoring those who died in Vietnam, but also providing an opportunity for Harley riders to get together and party. Harley riders all feel themselves to be members of a community of fellow Harley riders.

You would never consider showing up to "Rolling Thunder" (or a Hells Angels rally) riding a Yamaha.

All of us niche target marketers can learn important lessons on how to create a unique brand and a loyal following by studying the Grateful Dead and Harley-Davidson. Their approach was not to be all things to all people. It was not to try to broaden their audience. It was to stay narrow and to drill deep—to focus all attention on their most dedicated enthusiasts, to never take their following for granted, to keep feeding their customers more of what they want...and to ignore everyone else.

The Grateful Dead and Harley-Davidson stayed true to the 80/20 rule in marketing.

Chapter Seventy
Become part of your customer's regular routine

An iron law of marketing is that people are creatures of habit.

I always buy Crest toothpaste. I don't know why. I just always have, I guess because my mom bought Crest when I was a kid. I know I need toothpaste. I know this toothpaste works. And Crest is well known because of relentless advertising over many decades. It would take some effort to persuade me to switch to another toothpaste.

Other companies are spending billions of dollars to persuade people to use their toothpaste instead of Crest. But they aren't having much impact on me because I'm used to Crest. I'm comfortable with that brand.

People who have chosen to contribute to your organization or buy your product instead of your competitor's would prefer to stick with you. To switch their allegiance to another organization or comparable product is to admit that they had made a wrong decision—in effect, to admit failure. It's very difficult to change people's buying patterns, because this means moving people out of their comfort zone.

People are creatures of habit. But you will lose your customers if they lose sight of you—that is, if they stop receiving communications.

Or if they receive communications so infrequently that you are no longer a part of their regular routine, no longer a part of their everyday life.

Email makes it very inexpensive to stay in almost daily contact with your customers.

Your email communications should not all be sales pitches. Very few should be. Your email communications should provide valuable information that you know will be of interest to your customers.

You must constantly put your organization, your business, your service, your product, in front of your customers and leads—just like Nike, Coca-Cola, McDonald's, and every successful corporation that depends on the average consumer for business. This is such a basic principle of marketing that I am stunned at how few small businesses understand it.

Chapter Seventy-One
An easy way to reduce requests for refunds

The money-back guarantee is an essential staple of the mail order business. Especially if you are selling a big-ticket item, those who order will be subject to a natural human emotion known as "Buyer's Remorse."

"Did I really need that?" is a question that people will have. "Have I just been conned? Is this a waste of money? Will this product really do what the letter promises? Did I get a good price? Is this just another scam?"

To mitigate "Buyer's Remorse," follow-up the order with a letter, an email, and even a phone call aimed at reassuring your customer— who bought from you because she believed what you told her.

I'm sure you've asked these same questions yourself after buying something pricey.

Most refund requests come in right away—seldom weeks or months later. That's because "Buyer's Remorse" sets in right after the purchase and then fades over time, even if the customer isn't thrilled with your product. It's during those first few days immediately after the purchase that the threat of a refund request is most acute.

So your follow-up campaign after the purchase is very important. It's a critical marketing element ignored by most businesses.

Your letter should congratulate your customer on her purchase. Reassure her that she made the right decision. Your letter should restate the promises you've made and offer to help her if she has any trouble using your product. Encourage her to call you or her customer service representative if she's having any difficulty. Stay in communication with your customer to make sure the product is working as anticipated.

By following up like this, you will diffuse any anxieties and frustrations your customer might be having. Most importantly, you will begin to develop a relationship with your new customer that will set the stage for many more sales to this customer in the future.

Chapter Seventy-Two
Generating leads

Salespeople **will not survive** long if they are told to generate their own leads through cold calling. They will get discouraged, psychologically and emotionally worn down buy all the rejections. Sales people need leads. And they need good leads. Or you will lose your sales force.

If someone calls your office in answer to one of your lead generation letters, the chances are you've got a good lead. You have someone who's interested. You have someone who wants to talk. You have someone who has called you on his schedule, who is eager to chat, who is not being interrupted at the dinner hour by a telemarketer.

All calls that come into your office in answer to your letter are at least 10 times more likely to buy than a "cold call" prospect who wasn't looking for you and has never heard of you.

There are three basic categories of lead generation programs:

1) Business-to-consumer

The practicality of lead generation programs to consumers is dictated almost entirely by price point.

Lead generation programs make economic sense if you are selling big-ticket items, such as homes, mortgages, vacations, vehicles, landscaping, lawn care, legal services, insurance, or country club memberships.

Lead generation programs to consumers probably won't make sense for items under $50. For low-cost items (books, magazine subscriptions, kitchen gadgets, and the like) the first mailing will likely have to do all the selling.

When selling low-cost or low-margin items, it just becomes too costly to come at the prospect over and over again to get the sale, unless you have a lot of money to spend and can wait a long time to recover your investment.

A potentially cheap way to generate leads for your mailings to consumers is through the Internet. With the Internet, you don't have postage costs, paper costs, or printing costs. Internet marketing is different from direct mail in that with direct mail, your mailing reaches out to consumers, actually gets into their homes.

You can't do that on the Internet.

With the Internet you have to learn how to put bait out there. Your leads then have to find you.

Direct mail is more like hunting. With direct mail you go out and get the customer. You physically find the customer and drag him in the door, like slaying a wildebeest.

Internet marketing is more like fishing. You put your hook and bait in the water, and you wait for your customers and leads to come to you. And they will come if you have the right bait.

The Internet can be a wonderful lead generation tool if used skillfully.

2) Business-to-business

Lead generation programs should be a major feature of just about any marketing campaign directed toward business.

Nearly everything a business buys is almost by definition a big-ticket item.

Businesses buy even paper, pens, and paper clips in bulk.

So it's well worth investing a significant sum of money to land a successful business as a client or customer.

3) Public relations generated leads

This category is outside the scope of this book, but I'll mention it in passing. These are leads generated by news coverage and articles. People read about you in the *Wall Street Journal* and call, write, or track you down on the Internet. Free news coverage can produce a flood of leads and even orders. But I'm not covering it much here because this is a book about sales letters, not public relations, which is a different animal.

Also, generating news coverage is difficult to systematize and control. It's great when it happens, and there are steps you can take to increase the odds of receiving news coverage, but it's difficult to control or predict.

So that's all I'll say about public relations here.

Facts about "lead generation" that should interest you

Here is some data that might whet your appetite for putting in place a lead generation strategy:

- About 60% of all inquiries are made with the intention of buying your product or a similar product from your competitor. The question for these folks is not whether they will buy, but from whom they will buy.

- 53% of those inquirers who contact you, will also contact your competitor.

- 25% of those who have an "immediate need" will buy from the company that triggered the call with a mailing or advertisement.

- 20% of those who inquire and ask for information never receive any information. No one from the company ever follows up.

- Of those companies that do follow-up with information to the inquirer, 43% deliver the information too late to be of any use.

- 59% of inquirers say they threw away the information they received because it had nothing to do with why they had inquired and so was of no use.

- About 10% of inquiries are considered "hot leads"—meaning people who will buy immediately, either from you or your competitor.

These statistics, provided by Advertising Research Foundation, should encourage you in two ways. This data illustrates the enormous potential profitability of a lead generation program, and also reveals how inept most companies are at following up leads quickly.

The Lesson: If you launch a lead generation program, make sure you are set up to immediately answer and fulfill requests. Have your follow-up letters and packets ready. Make sure your sales team is prepared to swing into action.

Feeding your sales force

What's worse: too many leads or not enough?

That's really not the right question. The correct question is: What is a qualified lead? How do I assess the quality of the lead?

It's easy to generate inquiries. That's no problem at all. If I put out an ad that says "Free Sex! Call 1.800_____," I will get lots of calls, lots of interest—including probably from the police.

What your sales force wants are good leads—leads that have a real chance of buying. Nothing will discourage your sales team more than feeding them a lot of bad leads. The challenge is generating *qualified* inquiries.

One way to qualify a lead is not to bury the price of your product. Don't put the high price in a bright red banner headline. But include it somewhere in the literature you are sending, if there's a fixed price.

That way you will know those who answer your letter are not discouraged about the price. They are qualified leads.

If mentioning the price is not possible because of the nature of your service or business, another way to qualify your leads is to know who you are sending your lead generation letters to. You only write to those who can afford you, who are used to paying what you charge. The question then is not whether the prospect can afford you, but whether the prospect needs your service.

I will then use some kind of reply device the prospect would need to return to become qualified for a sales call.

Such a lead generation letter might look something like this:

Dear Mr. Smith:

If I could show how I can save you 20% over what you are paying now for your printing, would you be interested in meeting with me?

If your answer is yes, please return the enclosed reply card and I will call to set up a meeting.

The reason I am confident we can cut 20% off what you are paying now for your printing is because I know exactly what our competitors are charging.

Please be assured that our lower prices in no way mean lower quality. Quite the opposite.

Because we have just refitted our entire plant with brand new state-of the art web presses, your printing will be crisp and clear. In fact, if you ever find a problem with the quality of our printing, we'll print the order again for you at no charge.
I am very much hoping you will give us a chance to bid on your business.

I am anxious to receive your answer by return mail in the next few days.

Sincerely,

John Q. Sample
Vice President of Customer Service

P.S. The companies we've been meeting with
are stunned by how low our prices are. As a
result, our printing press schedule is nearly
full. So it's important we meet soon, within
the next week if possible, before we are
completely booked.

If you are not able to meet with me, I will
be very happy to meet with the person who
makes the decisions about your printing. In
that case, please just write the name of
the person I should talk with on the enclosed
reply card and mail it back to me. You can
also call me at **1.800.**_____. Thank you
so much.

Anyone who answers this letter is a great prospect. The conversation is started. The relationship has begun.

Notice that the letter does not promise a follow-up call in the event the reader does not respond. That's because the purpose of this letter is to qualify the lead. Of course, this letter does not rule out a follow-up call either.

If the reply card is returned, you might not get an order right away, but you have the green light to schedule a meeting. You have an opening to continue to send your prospect follow-up letters, information, announcements, invitations to social events, email communications, a newsletter, baseball tickets, whatever seems appropriate. The main thing is to keep the conversation going and to stay in front of your prospect. You now have a better-than-even chance of getting some business. And if your quality is good and if you keep your promises, you might be able to lock in another big account.

Follow-up your letter with a call

You will be far more successful with your lead generation and sales calls if you send a letter before you call. That way you are not a total stranger when your call comes in asking for a meeting.

One of the biggest mistakes marketers and sales people make is to rely on one shot—one letter or one call. The big advertisers (Nike,

McDonalds, Coke) know they must be in front of their market all the time. If you watch an hour of golf on TV, you might see ten Nike ads. You must keep yourself in front of your prospects continuously with interesting letters, emails, newsletters, faxes, and announcements. When they need your service, you want to be right there when they are making their decisions.

Give away a free steak

Morton's steakhouse sometimes sends me a letter offering me a free steak if I bring at least one person along and buy a dinner. I always take Morton's up on the offer because I love steak and Morton's is one of my favorite restaurants.

And of course, when I bring in my coupon and cash in on my free steak, I'm buying the second dinner for my guest. I'm buying wine. I'm buying side dishes. I'm buying coffee and I might buy dessert.

Even with the free steak, my bill for the night is still well over $100, so I don't think Morton's loses any money on me by tossing me a free steak. But far more important to Morton's is that I came to the restaurant. I would not have come that night without the offer of the free steak. I then will have a great experience and I will be more likely to think of Morton's when I'm in the mood for a steak and a nice dinner.

All kinds of stores and businesses can adopt this approach.

If you've just opened up a new deli in an office building, why not distribute a flier to every office in the building, perhaps in neighboring office buildings as well, and offer everyone a free sandwich who comes in before Tuesday, June 1.

Those who come in for the free sandwich will also buy a soda, a bag of chips, maybe a cup of coffee. So you aren't losing much. And if your sandwiches are great, you are gaining customers who will be coming back many, many times.

When I was a young direct mail copywriter trying to land a client, I would offer my prospect a risk-free mailing. If the mailing failed, the client would owe nothing. An offer like this requires confidence that my mailing will work. But I should not be in this business if I don't think my mailings will work. But here's the calculation I make: If just one in five of my mailings work, this is successful...because test mailings are relatively small compared to rollouts of successful tests.

And if a test works, the upside can be to mail millions of letters, sometimes many millions of letters.

So don't be afraid to let your prospects sample what you do for free. If your product or service is good, you won't lose money, you'll gain customers. Give away a free steak, a free trial subscription, free perfume, a free newsletter, a free stock tip, a free special report, a free mailing, free coffee, a free pastry, a free test-drive, a free lesson, a free seminar, free beer, a free wine tasting, a free cigar. It's an offer no intelligent person can refuse. And it might be your cheapest form of marketing.

Generate store traffic

Bookstores love to bring in a famous author with a new best-selling book for a book signing and maybe have her give a lecture. The author loves it because it helps her sell her new book. The bookstore loves it because it brings people into the store. Stores rely on traffic to generate business because most people in stores buy on impulse.

Creating attractive events is one of the best methods of generating traffic in your store. If you are an art gallery, have a free wine and cheese reception with the famous artist.

Here's a concept for a dealer in high-end cars: This could generate some great store traffic for a Lexus dealer, and could be especially effective mailed to prospects whose current car leases are on the verge of expiring.

You are cordially invited
to the

Annual Lexus Driving Exposition

You can test drive all our 2007 models
on our specially designed driving course.

Then cap off this extraordinary experience with
free golf tips from PGA pro [Big Name]
or a luxurious spa treatment.

September 9, 2006
9 a.m. to 6:00 p.m.

Hold a seminar

Holding a seminar in your area of expertise can be a great way to generate interest in your business, red-hot leads and clients. This approach can work well for financial planners; plastic surgeons; nutrition, wellness, health and medical centers; wealth-building programs; real estate; sales and marketing programs; business leadership and management; and other fields where specialized knowledge and expertise are at a premium.

I've gained many clients from among those who heard a speech I delivered or who attended a seminar I conducted. There seems to be an almost unlimited market for educational programs. People crave knowledge and information because gaining knowledge and information in your field is the key to getting where you want to go in life.

Chapter Seventy-Three
Generating referrals

Some businesses and organizations are built entirely through referrals. I'm a member of a public policy organization called the Council for National Policy that meets three times a year in nice locations around the country—Boca Raton, Aspen, Laguna Beach, places like that. The purpose of the organization is to connect successful business leaders with right-of-center public policy organizations and candidates.

The goal is to interest these business leaders and wealthy individuals in politics and public policy and to get them contributing money to these non-profit public policy organizations, as well as right-of-center candidates. The only way you can join this organization is to be nominated by another member.

You then have the privilege of paying a $2,500 membership fee every year, plus the fee for attending the three meetings. At these meetings you might hear from the President or Vice President of the United States, the Speaker of the House, the Senate Majority Leader and many other political leaders and luminaries. The attraction of membership in the Council is that you will have plenty of opportunity to meet with and talk with Republican Party leaders and other influential policy-makers. The Council is marketed as an exclusive organization. It's considered an honor to be invited to join.

I'm not sure it is an honor. But that's how it's sold. And the only way you can get in is with a referral from another member. You will then receive a letter announcing that you have been nominated for membership in the Council by so and so.

This strategy can be deployed effectively for all kinds of organizations and associations.

One of my clients is a creator of educational programs for high-achieving young people. The way we find students is to write to teachers and ask them to nominate six of their best students to participate in this prestigious National Young Leaders Conference.

The nominations come in from the teachers. The names and addresses of the student nominees are entered into a database. The nominees then receive a letter saying something like:

```
Congratulations!

    I am pleased to announce that you have
been nominated to be a National Scholar
and Delegate to _____ in
Washington, D.C., this fall.

    Your teacher, [Name], identified you as
one of [School Name]'s most outstanding
students. The Nominations Committee then
examined your academic record and concluded
that you qualify for nomination.

    You should feel proud of your exemplary
academic record and your selection to be
a National Scholar representing the state
of Virginia.
```

The letter is sent out in an impressive-looking invitation holder. The package looks a lot like a wedding invitation. It includes a program schedule, an impressive list of advisors, a letter from President Bush welcoming the students and an Enrollment Application. Another letter is sent to the parents at the same time. The tuition for the five-day conference is about $1,400.

The point is, this list is developed by way of a referral strategy. The students are found by asking teachers to give us the names of their best students. This is how the prospect (invitation) list is built.

When this letter arrives, it has instant credibility because the teacher's name is mentioned right away. If this child's teacher is involved in this program, it must be worthwhile. This will be very powerful evidence for the parent of the value of the program.

This is a potent way to use the referral strategy.

But many businesses and salesmen can use this same strategy to improve their marketing.

Ask your clients to do you a favor by giving you the names and addresses of three or five friends or people they know who can benefit from your product or service, and should be using it.

You can then begin your letter to your referred lead something like this.

Dear Mr. Smith,

I was talking with your friend Steve Jones yesterday and he mentioned to me that you might need life insurance.

Steve and I are long-time friends. He is also a life insurance policyholder of mine and has been for more than 10 years.

I would very much welcome meeting with you to discuss your insurance situation.

Even if you own some life insurance already, I would like to talk with you about some recent changes in the tax law that affect life insurance -- changes that might require you to restructure some of your affairs to avoid a large additional tax bite that you might not be anticipating.

We also have some very interesting new products that might allow you to protect your estate and shelter a significant portion of your assets from being taken by the IRS.

I would very much like to meet with you at your convenience, but the sooner the better.

I can be reached anytime, either at my office number, which is _____ or on my cell phone, which is _____.

If I don't hear from you in the next few days, I hope you won't mind if I give you a call to see if we can schedule a meeting.

Can you see how much stronger a referred name is than simply writing to a cold name?

Not only is the referred name a qualified lead, because his friend knows he's looking for life insurance, or has a need for more life insurance. But your prospecting letter, even though you have never met this person, is attention-getting, because the first line mentions the friend you both have in common. So you already have a bond, a connection. And the letter is far more credible, because your prospect can easily check with your friend to get your friend's assessment of you and your service.

Your client and friend, who you know is very happy with you, will say great things about you, further strengthening your marketing.

Does this ensure you will get a sale from this prospect? Of course not, but the odds are now exponentially more in your favor.

And the referral strategy can be replicated over and over again. The more clients you have, the more referrals you can collect and mail. The key is simply to ask your happy clients for the names of others they know who can use your service.

Your referral strategy can become a systematized program.

Chapter Seventy-Four
Conduct surveys to find qualified leads

Surveys are great tools to use in the right situation.

Surveys are, in fact, a great tool to use if you are in the lead generation business or if you are offering a wide range of products and services.

The purpose of the survey is simply to ask your prospect what he wants, what he's interested in—and then sell him what he's just told you he wants.

This is what politicians do.

President Clinton, and his advisors, were obsessed with conducting surveys and focus groups to find out what voters were thinking, what was on their minds, what they wanted. And then Clinton would craft his message exactly according to what the polls were telling him and his speechwriters.

President Clinton was a master politician. He was a master marketer and salesman. His approach was scientific. The survey data came in. He crafted his message accordingly.

We can do the same thing in all our marketing and sales work. We can conduct surveys both to find qualified prospects, and also to help us zero in more accurately on what our existing customers want.

Another great feature of surveys is that people like filling them out. People love an opportunity to give their opinions about things. You can also offer a reward for those who fill out and return your survey—perhaps a free special report on a subject you know is of interest to your reader.

A well-crafted letter and survey to a decent list should be able to get a 15 percent or even a 20 percent response rate.

The answers you get back from your surveys should then be organized and entered into a database.

Let's say you are selling a variety of health products. Health care expenses account for about one-seventh of the entire U.S. economy, so the virtue of this field is that everyone is interested in their health. Everyone has concerns about health, the quality of health care, the cost of health care, and government policy on health care.

And most people will be interested to complete a survey on their health care if they believe their participation in the survey might lead to better health, lower health care costs and a longer, healthier life. Senior citizens are especially concerned about health care. So you might start by targeting your letter to the over-60 crowd.

Here's how you might begin your letter, the goal being to persuade your reader to fill out and return your survey:

National Research Survey
On America's Health Care Needs and Concerns

```
Dear Mrs. Jones,

    You have been specially selected to
participate in this National Research
Survey on America's Health Care Needs and
Concerns.
```

The results of this survey will be submitted in a report to Congress and the President of the United States.

I am hoping you will take just a few minutes of your time to complete this important research poll.

Your participation will help ensure that your voice is counted and heard as the President and Congress prepare to reform Medicare and change how health care is delivered in America.

The results of this survey report will also be submitted to America's leading pharmaceutical companies and medical research institutions.

In addition, all participants in this survey will receive a free copy of the final survey report.

Your individual answers will be held in confidence. Only the overall results will be made public.

We have selected 355,000 citizens from across America to participate in this poll, representing every congressional district.

Because this survey is so large, you can be sure Congress and the White House will study the results carefully, and it will have a major impact on the Medicare and health care debate in Congress over the coming months, when crucial decisions on Medicare and the delivery of health care will be made.

So I hope you will make a special point of completing and returning your survey for processing today.

The survey letter starts this way because you must give your reader some compelling reasons to take the time and effort to fill out and return the survey.

The incentive in this case is the promise of having an impact on the health care and Medicare reform debate taking place in Congress.

The incentive is having one's voice heard and counted by the powerful—important decision-makers whose decisions will have a major impact on all of our lives.

People vote in elections because they want their voice, their opinion to count. People will fill out a survey like this for the same reason.

The letter will continue to develop these points. The survey questions then become very important. The survey should begin with a series of public policy issue questions concerning Medicare and health care delivery in America, questions along the lines of:

- Do you think Medicare should be changed to be a program only for those who can't afford health insurance?

- Are you in favor of more government control over health care, or less?

- Do you believe government should guarantee health care for all Americans?

- How do you rate the overall quality of health care in America?

- Are you for or against the President's proposal to...?

- Would you like to see Congress make all your medical and health care expenses tax-deductible?

After you complete the public policy questions, you start to move into more personal questions.

- What is your age range?

- What is your income range?

- Approximately how much do you spend on medical treatment each year?

- How much do you spend on prescription drugs each year?

- How much do you spend on vitamins each year?

- How much do you spend on supplements each year?

- Which prescription drugs do you use most?

- Do you now have health insurance?

- How concerned are you about the quality of your current coverage?

- What is your weight?

- What is your height?

- Do you belong to a gym or health club?

- How much exercise do you do each week?

- What kinds of regular exercise do you focus on?

- How do you rate your overall health?

And there are all kinds of other related questions you might ask, depending on the information you need. Can you see how the answers to such questions could be very helpful to a marketer selling health products?

Your survey should be an impressive, official-looking document; a four-page booklet at a minimum. I sometimes construct eight-page surveys. Your survey should look like it might have been produced by a government agency, perhaps the Census Bureau, or an academic or medical research institution. The survey should look prestigious.

And, as you promised in your letter, you will deliver an impressive report to Congress and the White House on the results of the survey, which truly can have an impact on the policy debate.

You do everything you say you will do with the survey, including delivering a copy of the final report to all who participated.

You now have an enormous number of great leads for your health-related products. The value of these leads will then be determined by your "conversion rate"—that is, what percentage of leads become customers. It then becomes a mathematical equation how much you can spend to acquire a lead.

Of course, your "conversion rate" will be affected dramatically, up or down, by the quality of your survey questions, the products you are selling and the skill of your conversion campaign. The quicker you follow up with your conversion program, the more productive your leads.

As you can see, I'm a huge fan of the survey as a marketing tool.

Chapter Seventy-Five
Google AdWords

I'm having a lot of fun with this amazing tool, an incredibly powerful engine for generating leads and testing messages and themes. And it does not require a lot of money if you proceed cautiously and correctly.

I've become a bit of a Google AdWords junky.

I'll summarize how it works. You'll have to try it for yourself and do a lot of tinkering with this tool before you will begin to understand how to make it work for you.

You can waste a lot of money if you aren't careful.

So here's how it works.

People go to the Internet to find information about subjects or to find products. What they do is type "key words" into Google on their browser. They then wait a few seconds and see what pops up.

Google is the world's most popular search engine. Almost everyone uses Google for searches. And Google powers the searches for many other lesser search engines as well, including AOL, Ask

Jeeves, EarthLink, Hot Bot, and others.

What Google does is allow you to bid on key words and phrases. The key words you've selected and bid on are then linked by Google to mini-ads Google allows you to create (in Google's format) for display on searches of the key words you've selected for your ads. Your ads are linked to your Web site, or the Web site you've created for the product you are selling.

There are some important tricks to making Google AdWords work.

Trick #1

Select narrow key words and phrases that describe exactly what you are selling. If your key words are too broad or too popular, you will spend a fortune to get your ad listed high enough in searches to have any impact.

The key word "computers" would not be a good key word for most of us because then you would be going up against Dell, Microsoft, and the huge computer companies. And there are so many companies selling computers, especially on the Internet, that you will get lost, like a grain of sand on a beach.

What you want to use Google AdWords for is a specialized product. Suppose, just for fun, you test the keyword "Iguana."

According to Google, I can have a near monopoly on the word "Iguana" for almost nothing. And, according to Google's "Traffic Estimator" function, I will be the very first listing for about 10 cents a click for anyone looking for information on Iguanas.

Also, according to Google's "Traffic Estimator" function, there seem to be quite a lot of people searching for information on Iguanas. Why is that?

Well, I did not know this before, but it turns out the Iguana is a popular pet. More importantly, people who own an Iguana as a pet, love their Iguanas, are Iguana fanatics. These Iguana owners worry about the health of their Iguana. They want a healthy Iguana so their Iguana can live a long, healthy and happy life.

So a plausible business strategy is to craft a product, specifically designed for Iguana owners, perhaps a book titled something like: "Make Your Iguana a Healthy, Happy, Long-living Iguana."

Judging by the number of clicks I see estimated for the keyword "Iguana," my guess is someone could make a healthy profit producing just such a book and using Google AdWords to market it.

Google AdWords is a great tool for entrepreneurs and marketers to reach niche markets with highly targeted and specialized niche products.

Trick #2

Make sure the Web site your Google ads are linked to are precisely on point with the key words you've bought and the subject of your ad. Do not link you ads to your general site, which might be offering many services and products. Link your ad to a Web site and response or order form specifically designed for your key word and Google ad.

Trick #3

Test different headlines on your ad. You'll find an enormous difference in the number of clicks and inquiries generated by the various headlines you test. I picked the title of this book based on the headline and key word that was working best on the Google AdWord system. Turns out quite a lot of people want to learn how to write effective sales and lead generation letters. "Sales Letters" is a key word phrase that is typed into searches a lot. I found I could be listed #1 in the search for about 20 cents a click. And I found that the ad headline "Great Sales Letters" attracted the most clicks. Google only allows very short headlines on ads, a maximum of 25 characters. So you have to really boil your message down—a great exercise for ad writers.

Interestingly, I found that the headline "Great Sales Letters" pulled about ten times more clicks than "Great Sales Copywriter." What a great reminder to me that what my prospects care about is the product—or more precisely the end result. People don't care one wit about me. They did not want a "great sales copywriter" to help them. They wanted great sales letters. How they get the letters is unimportant. But then I found that "Blockbuster Sales Letters" Pulled even better than "Great." So that's how I picked the title for this book.

Trick #4

Do not become obsessed with the number of clicks your ads attract. I can always design an ad that will generate an avalanche of clicks. But that will just cost you a ton of money. That's great for Google, but not for you. What counts are quality clicks. What counts is how many clicks turn into inquiries, and how many inquiries are converted into sales.

Trick #5

What Google wants are lots of clicks. What Google wants is for you to pay a high cost for each click on your ad and Web site because that's how Google makes money. So Google will cancel your ad if it's not making enough money for Google. And Google will keep moving your ad down the listing (until it disappears, or nearly disappears) if your ad is not attracting traffic. If you pay a lot per click, and if your ad is okay, you can stay high on the Google key word search listing. But that's not what you want. You want to pay as little as possible per click, and have a high percentage of your clicks turn into sales. You also want enough traffic to keep Google happy, that is to keep your ad listed first, or very high up in listings for the key words you've chosen. So your job is to select key words, to then design ads for those key words that will allow you to attract quality clicks, a high enough percentage of which will become customers, at as low a cost as possible. And don't forget to link your ad to a Web page that is exactly on message.

The Brilliance of Google AdWords

A great benefit of the Google AdWords system is that you can test ideas, words, and phrases in minutes. I can find out what's working and not working. When I'm writing a sales or marketing letter designed for print, I'll often go into Goggle AdWords to experiment with different headlines, phrases, and key words—just to see what pulls best.

But the best way to learn how to use Google AdWords successfully is to go there and just start playing with it. You will make mistakes. You will waste some money, as I certainly did and continue to do with all my experimenting. But it will be money well spent, because you will learn a lot about marketing and human psychology by how people respond to your ads on Google.

Google AdWords is like a stern teacher that slaps my wrist with a ruler every time I break the laws of marketing. The system forces me to tailor my product, my service to the market, not to try to mold the market to fit my product. It forces me to sell people what they are asking me for with their key word searches and clicks.

That's why I'm such a Google AdWord junky.

Yahoo has a similar tool called Overture. But I have not found it nearly as productive as Google AdWords. What an awesome company Google is! I just hope Google does not ruin AdWords by becoming too greedy and charging too much.

Chapter Seventy-Six
Offer a free report

Remember what I said about Internet marketing being more like fishing, direct mail marketing being more like hunting?

To be a good fisherman, you need the right bait. You put the bait on the hook and wait until the fish bite.

Whether you are using Google AdWords, Yahoo Overture or banner ads on sites related to your product, your goal is to capture email addresses of people who are interested in your product, or something like your product. More accurately, you want those who have a problem that can be addressed or fixed by your product.

An effective way to entice people to give you their email address is to offer them in return a free special report that is exactly on the topic of their interest. The special report should not be an ad. The special report should be valuable information your prospect will be very pleased to receive.

If the special report is a quality product in its own right, you have the potential of capturing a lot of email addresses of qualified leads. And the leads you capture will be very happy with what they receive. You will be developing a valuable list of prospects—a percentage of whom can become customers.

Offering something free that your target audience wants is a great way to capture email addresses. But be sure what you are giving away is precisely in line with what you are selling. Morton's steakhouse gave me a free steak as an enticement for me to go to the restaurant.

Offering me free gasoline would have been a waste of money and effort for Morton's. By offering a free steak, Morton's is sure it is attracting steak lovers.

Chapter Seventy-Seven

You can't sell without the right list

Not enough attention is paid to lists by direct mail marketers.

In fact, I know of no one in my profession who spends enough time on lists—including me.

The list, or list segment, you select for your mailing is far more important than the letter itself.

The list—that is, the qualified prospects you are trying to sell to—is the single most important element of your marketing campaign. It's possible for a poorly written letter to work to a good list. But it's impossible for a fantastic letter to work to the wrong list. The list is not just a way to reach your market. It is your market.

I'll discuss lists for your prospecting program first, then your program to your customer list—your "housefile."

Lists for prospecting

I have covered a number of lead generation strategies earlier, so I won't be getting back into lead generation programs much here. In this section, I will mostly focus on lists you can rent.

The mailing list business is an enormous industry. There are approximately 30,000 lists available for rental. There are about one billion names on these lists.

If you wonder why you receive so much mail every day from businesses, charities, political causes, and candidates all wanting you to send money for something, it's because your name and address is being rented by list owners, list managers, and list brokers. Your name is being rented or sold, most likely because you bought something through the mail or you contributed to some cause in response to a letter.

Once you're on a mailing list, it's very difficult to get off, because your name and address is being sold and rented to dozens of organizations and businesses. You would have to not answer a piece of junk mail for about three years before you started to see a noticeable decline in the amount of commercial and fundraising mail in your mailbox.

You would also have to not buy anything over the Internet, not use your credit card, not subscribe to any magazines, and not fill out any forms that ask for your contact information at stores. In addition, you would need to move to a poor neighborhood. If you live in a wealthy neighborhood, you'll receive a lot of direct mail just because direct mail marketers know you have money to spend.

What you're looking to rent are lists of folks who have bought the same kind of product you are selling. If you are selling exercise equipment, rent lists of people who have recently bought exercise equipment, because you know these people are interested in fitness. If you are selling gardening products, rent lists of people who regularly buy gardening products.

In the direct mail business you typically do not buy a mailing list. You rent a list for a one-time use. If you want to mail to the list again, you must rent it again. But anyone who answers your letter becomes part of your customer list—or housefile. In other words, the name is now yours and you are free to continue to send letters to that person without renting that name again. But you are not permitted to continue to mail letters to those who do not respond to your prospect appeal unless you rent the list again.

What you want are buyers who have bought a lot of what you are selling—multi-buyers. And you want buyers who have bought something recently, within the last six or 12 months.

You might need to pay more for these premium names, but it will almost always be worth it. I would much rather pay more for names that I know will be good than less for names that I'm unsure of.

The more recent the purchase, the better the prospect.

This is an important point, worth underscoring, because it's counterintuitive. You might think these would be the weakest prospects on the assumption that these buyers might be tapped out since they just bought. But these recent hotline frequent buyers are, by far, the most likely to answer your letter with an order.

Those who have not bought anything, at least as far as you know, for a long time are weak prospects.

Once you build a sizeable customer list, you'll then have some clout to start negotiating name-exchange agreements with marketers who sell similar products, and this can help you save money on list rental fees. A name exchange is when you allow one marketer to mail to your list of buyers in exchange for that organization or business letting you mail its list of buyers.

A great living can be made by just learning lists. Learn everything about lists. Attend seminars on lists. Learn all the list jargon and terms, so you don't sound like an amateur when ordering lists.

Think about lists all the time. Ask about lists. Subscribe to every direct mail marketing publication, such as *DM News* and *Direct Marketing* magazine where you will find countless ads from list companies advertising their lists. Become a member of the Direct Marketing Association. And make a special point to attend direct mail marketing seminars, which are offered all the time by the Direct Marketing Association.

Many mailing lists can be found through the Standard Rate and Data Service, which publishes the *SRDS Direct Marketing List Source.*

This service will tell you what lists are available on the open market, describe the list, and tell you who to contact to rent a list. SRDS breaks down lists into many different categories for direct mail business offers and fundraising solicitations.

The Marketing Information Network (MIN) offers more than 20,000 lists online. Dun & Bradstreet compiles lists of businesses and the executives of these businesses. D&B also compiles lists of individuals by profession.

There are many list services and list brokers. You should find a reputable list broker to help you who specializes in the market you are trying to reach.

Be open to hand-compiling your own lists, especially for highly targeted appeals that hold out promise of a big return on investment and not just relying on renting lists that are on the open market. Become a list maniac.

Here are some crucial points to keep in mind when conducting your list work for your prospecting program.

1. Be crystal clear in your list orders.

A mistake in the way you order names can be catastrophic. It's very easy to fall into direct mail jargon, and then discover later that different people attach different meanings to the jargon. When ordering a list from a list broker or an organization, write your order very clearly, precisely, and in plain English. Find out what terms they use and exactly what each term means. Get on the phone with the list broker and go over your written list order verbally, line by line, word by word. Assume nothing.

Make sure you understand exactly what kind of names you are getting for your mailing. Get everything in writing. If you're not sure what their terms mean, get clarification IN WRITING.

2. Learn how to read a list data card.

Even if you use a list broker, you will still be making the decisions as to what kinds of names you want to order from particular lists for your mailing.

Learn how to read a list data card. This is jargon that means a sheet of paper that describes a particular list and what segments are available for rent. Each data card includes a paragraph or two about the background of the list and how the list was compiled. You will want to know what percentage of the list is direct mail generated. You will want to know the precise product and service offers that built the list.

Understand the terms and the selects available for rent. In general, the more name selection options available the better. You may be able to select not only according to buying history and date of most recent purchase, but also by frequency of purchase, gender, age, geographic region and income level.

Pay careful attention to what kinds of businesses and organizations have rented a list you are considering, and especially which ones have rolled out or mailed a continuation with this list. Were the product offers similar to yours?

If so, this is probably a good list to test. If you see a lot of tests but few continuations, this is likely a weak list.

Question every list's hygiene. Ask how often the list is updated and corrected. Many list suppliers will guarantee the cleanliness of their lists and refund postage costs on letters returned (called pixies or nixies) in excess of some reasonable percentage. About 15 percent of the population moves every year, so lists go out of date very quickly. Ask tough questions about the hygiene of lists you're renting. Try hard to get guarantees of list cleanliness in writing.

Another important factor to consider is the direct mail techniques used to build the list you're considering renting. For example, some lists are built mainly on sweepstakes offers and are therefore not likely to be strong prospect lists for a conventional sales appeal. Others are built mostly on front-end free gifts. Ask the list supplier about the kinds of packages that built the list.

And always test before you roll out, especially on a list which you have not used recently. Often lists can appear very similar from their data card descriptions but will yield radically different results. The data card descriptions will guide your initial decision to test a list, along with guidance from the experienced list broker you've hired. But only your test results can dictate whether you continue or roll out on a list.

3. Find a great list broker.

List brokers are a great resource. List brokers are paid on commission. Usually they take a 20 percent commission on names they find and supply for you. This commission is paid by the list owner, not you. You would typically pay the same for a list whether or not you use a list broker—though, as in real estate transactions, this can also be negotiated.

You want to make sure your list broker is paid well, and that your relationship is a profitable one for the broker. Good list brokers are worth their weight in gold.

Be sure you select a list broker who specializes in the market you're trying to reach. If you're selling a newsletter subscription, don't use a list broker who specializes in product catalogues.

But don't rely on your list broker to make decisions. Your list broker only makes recommendations. You and only you will make your final list decisions. So even if you have a list broker, you should still make a habit of collecting and studying List Data Cards.

4. Try to negotiate "net-net" payment terms on prospect lists.

As your business grows, you will find it more and more difficult to rent lists that don't have a high rate of duplication with your own customer list, especially if you are in a small niche market. In a net-net name arrangement, you only pay for the name once and only pay for names that are not on your list. And you agree to mail only to unique names.

Some list owners won't agree to a pure net-net arrangement.

In the alternative, ask for a modified net-net deal. For example, you might ask for a net-net deal up to a maximum of 40 percent off the price of the list. Be creative in how you negotiate for renting lists. Use your imagination to get the best possible deal on prospect names.

5. Ask to exchange lists for a one-time use.

This is a great way to cut the cost of your prospect mailing.

The idea here is that you want to be able to mail to the customer lists of businesses that sell similar products to the products you are selling. And they will probably want to mail their offers to your customers. Negotiate a list exchange.

But be sure you are exchanging the same kind of names. Someone who is a frequent buyer is far more valuable than a one-time buyer. And someone who has paid $100 for something is more valuable than someone who has paid $20 for something. And a recent buyer is a better prospect than someone who has not bought anything in a long while. So make sure you're trading apples for apples, not apples for apple skins.

6. Pay attention to lists that are growing quickly.

The best prospects are those that have bought something recently. A rapidly growing list will contain a large portion of brand new buyers who likely will not have been pounded with direct mail offers from the organization you are renting from. Fast-growing lists, if on point, can be strong lists for your prospect program.

7. Tailor letters to the lists you're mailing.

Most direct mailers mail one-size-fits-all prospect packages. This is especially so when one has found a control package. The "control" package is direct mail jargon for an organization's most successful prospect package. A prospect package is a control package if it's successful and is beating all other prospect packages. When another package proves more successful, it becomes the new control.

But once you have a successful prospect package, make adjustments in the copy to appeal to specific lists and audiences. When you acquire a list, you are gaining access to a market. Each list has its own unique characteristics.

People on a list are united by a particular interest. Your letter should be written to take that interest into account. For example, you might be writing a letter to people who are subscribers to a certain magazine. Reference the magazine in the first few lines of your letter to show you know something about the person to whom you are writing. You'll need to get the list owner's permission to do this.

8. Test various segments of a list.

Often I hear direct mailers say that a list they tested did not work. I then find out that they only conducted one 5,000-name test of 0-to-18-month buyers from the list. Maybe this select from this list doesn't work. But narrowing your select to 0-to-6 month buyers might work just fine. Or maybe the list owner will let you mail to multi-buyers only, which are at least three times stronger than one-time buyers.

You should also conduct gender tests. Women and men respond differently. Some products, even if they are not gender specific products (insurance, for example) might nevertheless appeal more to women, or more to men. A list that might not work well if you mail both to men and women might work if you mail your appeal to just women or just men, depending on the product.

Geography can also make a difference. If you are selling Bibles, maybe your offer will work best in "Bible Belt" states. If you are selling gun-related products, maybe you should stick to rural areas, where there are a lot of hunters. Test to find out. You should also test by age and income if possible. The point is to not assume a list is no good for you just because your test of one broad select failed. Be surgical in your testing. Find out every select the list owner will let you test. Choose a series of intelligent tests.

You'll likely have to pay more for detailed and narrow selects, but the bigger return may well be worth the extra cost. And don't just accept what's printed on the data card as the only selects available. Negotiate the selects you want with the list owner. Be a strategist. Come at the prospect list you're renting from many different angles.

9. Repackage successful appeals and re-mail them to the same lists.

Successful packages can often be repackaged with different techniques, carriers, formats, and graphics and re-mailed through prospect lists that have worked well.

People remember how packages look, not so much the specific words that are in a package. By putting otherwise identical packages in different clothes, such as different looking envelopes, different colors, different paper stock, different graphic layout, most of your readers will assume it's a different letter.

As always, however, be sure to test your different look packages. A change in the way a package looks can dramatically affect returns, up or down. For example, I was using a yellow post-it note very successfully for a prospect appeal I had been mailing for months. I then tried using a light blue post-it note instead, just to change the look and to see if color was important. My returns dropped 25 percent. In this case, keeping the post-it note yellow was important, I guess because it looked more like a standard yellow post-it note people are used to seeing.

So make changes to the look and feel of your successful prospect packages. Constantly experiment. And always test your changes.

10. Beware of list owners who load your test with good names and give you garbage for your rollout.

You will occasionally run into the dishonest list owner who gives you gold-plated names (for example, 60-day hotline or multi-buyers) for your 5,000-letter prospect test. This produces dishonestly tremendous results on your test. You then order the rest of the names in the select you think you tested. Your 100,000-letter rollout then crashes because the broker sent you weaker names than you tested, perhaps threw in all the non-donors and people who may not have contributed in years. This can be a financial catastrophe. It's an old scam.

What can you do about this?

Answer: Not much, except make sure you're using a great list broker who knows the lists she's recommending and knows who the charlatans are. Very few list owners will pull this scam on you because they want a good reputation so that marketers will continue to rent their lists in the future. If you're in the business of renting lists, nothing will kill your business faster then getting a reputation for loading up tests. It would be like a casino cheating people. It wouldn't be long before no one showed up to play at that casino any more.

Still, there are a few steps you can take that will minimize your risk.

One is to roll out in stages. Never take for your rollout more than five times the number of names you tested. Another strategy I used with a list owner who I knew was loading up tests was only to order tests, never rollouts. That way I knew I was only getting the very best names, often getting 15 percent response rates on the test names he supplied.

I always look at test results very carefully. If I notice something out of the ordinary, such as a very high response rate, or a higher-than-expected average contribution, I'll order another 5,000 or 10,000 names in the same select and test again.

11. Beware of the incorrectly run select.

A related problem is ordering one select and getting something else, not because the list owner was dishonest but was just sloppy and made a mistake.

This happens sometimes, and errors are not easy to prove. Again, there's not a whole lot you can do, except ask your list broker to raise holy heck with the list owner.

Over time, as you gain experience with the lists you use most often, you will learn to spot out-of-the-ordinary results. Mostly, you'll just have to be guided by your experience. You'll learn the characteristics of many of the lists you'll be mailing. And you'll know in your gut that something just isn't right.

12. If the list owner rents you a test, be sure your purchase order includes a written agreement to let you roll out to the balance of the list.

One nasty trick some list owners pull is to make a little extra money by letting you test a list, but then deny your order to roll out to the list later. Often this happens when list owners notice your letter is too competitive with something they're doing. List owners will then sometimes steal your idea for their mail program.

The way to prevent this from happening is to state in writing on your purchase order that granting permission to test a list includes an agreement to allow a rollout to the list within 60 days of the test if the test is successful.

13. If you're prospecting with a non-sweepstakes offer, require the list owner to remove all "sweeps-only" buyers.

Some marketers have built a large portion of their house list with sweepstakes offers. An offer that uses a sweepstakes contest to draw the reader into the letter is a powerful marketing technique. But responders to sweepstakes offers tend to answer only offers built around a sweepstakes contest and are weak prospects for conventional marketing packages. It's fine if a buyer has answered both sweepstakes and conventional offers. What you don't want are sweeps-only or unique-sweeps buyers if you're mailing a conventional sales pitch. This little instruction can make an enormous difference in the performance of your prospecting campaign.

Remember, smart direct mailers spend a lot of time weeding out people who are least likely to respond. Sweeps-only buyers are not likely to answer your conventional sales offer. Weed them out.

Managing your customer list

Your customer list is the lifeblood of your business. Your customer, or house list, is the result of all your marketing efforts. Your house list is your moneymaker.

These people have shown with their orders and purchases that they like what you're selling. Here are some crucial rules and procedures for managing your customer list.

1. Set up a computerized database.

Some organizations do this themselves. Others maintain their database at a professional database maintenance company. If you decide to do this yourself, there are some off-the-shelf computer programs designed specifically to help you set up your own customer list. What you do will depend on the size and complexity of your database.

Setting up and maintaining a large database of buyers and customers can be an enormous, highly technical task that requires software, a data-entry system, and skilled computer technicians who understand marketing.

2. Set up your order-taking and data entry system.

If you are a mail order business, envelopes must be picked up at the post office, opened, checks deposited, and information entered into your database. This is called "batching and caging" in direct mail jargon. You will also be taking orders over the phone and over the Internet. There are large companies that specialize in taking your orders for you. But if you are a small operation, you might also do this yourself.

The critical point here is that you will need to set up a system for getting all the necessary information (names, postal addresses, email addresses, order amounts, products ordered, number of units orders, and any other pertinent pieces of information) into your computer database. Making sure this information is entered accurately into your database is absolutely critical to the success of your business.

Think of it this way: I might spend $25 (in prospect losses) to find a new $50+ buyer. If the name of the customer is incorrectly spelled by the data entry person, my investment in finding this new customer is greatly diminished, if not completely lost. Certainly my ability to conduct a highly personalized marketing campaign to that person is destroyed. Wrong personalization is worse than no personalization in your letter. Data-entry errors are very costly to your business.

One way I guard against this is to have the name and address entered in the computer twice. If the information is entered exactly the same way both times, we assume it's correct. This is called double data-entry verification.

This procedure might double the cost of your data entry but will be well worth the added cost. As an alternative, you might also consider partial double data-entry verification for your low-dollar customers, in which only the name of the buyer and zip code are entered twice. It's most important to get the name exactly right. The post office can usually deliver the mail even if the address is slightly off.

Other steps to cut down on data-entry errors include "finder number" and barcode scanning systems, which I won't get into here. These systems also have their shortcomings.

I'm always looking for ways to cut down on these costly mistakes. Data-entry errors are one of the biggest problems in direct marketing.

3. Collect as much useable information on your donors as you can.

The most important information you'll need to collect is the product ordered, the number of units ordered, the amount paid, the date of the order, the offer that generated the order and the list the order came from. This will allow you to know what product and offer your customer liked, and will allow you to tailor your future offers to what you now know he likes.

You need a coding system to keep track of what offers your customers answered. The codes for each mailing go on the order or reply form.

You should also strive to collect as much personal information as you can on your buyers, especially your best buyers.

You might ask for birthdays and the names of their family members as part of a survey. You'll be able to write far more personal appeals if you have this information. You'll dazzle your reader if you're able to ask how members of their family are doing and reference their actual names. Your customers will be amazed if you remember their birthdays and send a birthday card. Obviously, you can't afford this level of personal treatment for someone who has bought a $15 item once. But it's worth knowing this information on someone who's spending $1,000 or more with you every year.

You'll also want to ask for phone numbers, fax numbers, and email addresses. And be sure you know the gender of each customer and their proper title (Mr., Mrs., Ms., Miss, Dr., Father, Reverend, etc.). Gender is important because women and men respond differently to different approaches, even if the product you are selling is gender-neutral. And getting the title right is as important as getting the rest of the name right.

Try to find out what name they use in casual conversation. The name might be James, but the person might go by Jim. You should know the person's familiar name to make your communications more personal.

Each bit of information should be contained in its own separate field on your database so that you can retrieve it piecemeal and as needed. A copywriter must be familiar with all information available on a database to write an effective, highly personal letter that will sound like you know the person. The more information you have on your customers, the more personal you can make your letters.

This will dramatically improve the performance of your mailings and marketing efforts. But make sure the information you're collecting for your database is useable in your letters, for segmenting your list, and for the overall management of your marketing efforts. Have a specific, well-thought-out purpose for every piece of information you are collecting.

I've seen organizations go overboard in collecting data on customers they will never use. This is just a waste of money and makes your database unmanageable.

4. Make sure there aren't duplicate names in your database.

There are few things more annoying to your customers than receiving multiple copies of the same mailing on the same day. Talk about destroying your attempt to make your letter as personal as possible!

Computer programs can identify likely duplicates, but they aren't perfect.

For example, a computer program can identify two records where the name is spelled differently but is at the same address as a likely duplicate. For your best customers, perhaps the best 20 percent of your file, a human eye should examine the records, printed out in alphabetical order, to identify not just possible duplicate records, but other potential problems with the data that only a human eye and brain with the capacity to make judgments will notice.

You should not rely exclusively on a computer program to keep your housefile list clean, especially your top 10 percent or 20 percent of your customers. It's well worth the effort and cost to examine the records of your best customers with human eyes.

5. Steps to keep your housefile list clean and accurate.

Be a fanatic about the hygiene of your housefile list. And I mean a nut case. There are few things more important to the success of your direct mail marketing program.

Running your list through a National Change of Address (NCOA) program at least every six months will help. NCOA is a constantly updated database generated by the U.S. Postal Service. About 15 percent of Americans change their address every year, and any list loses about 50 percent of its value every two years if it's not "NCOAed."

Your reply forms should always include an instruction to your reader in red to "Please make any necessary corrections to your name and address on this reply form." Be sure any corrections your customers write on reply forms are entered into your database.

Verify names and addresses during telemarketing calls, and make sure the changes are made in your database. Undeliverable first-class mail will be returned to you by the post office. These are called nixies or pixies in direct mail jargon. Remove the bad addresses after making every effort to correct the bad addresses. You can also print "Address Correction Requested" on your carrier envelopes and, for a fee, the post office will correct a high percentage of wrong addresses. This service can be costly, so do this perhaps only twice a year.

Send out questionnaires periodically to your customers asking them to verify and correct the information you have on them. Questionnaires provide a great opportunity to update and correct errors in your database, and also to ask other questions that will help you in your marketing. Consider offering some incentive to your supporters, such as a gift or special report, for every questionnaire completed and returned.

Standardizing formats, merging multiple files, eliminating duplicates, and updating and verifying addresses also are all essential to keeping your house list productive. Failure to keep your list clean and accurate can and probably will bankrupt you quickly.

6. Establish your "unduping" policy.

I do not want my best customers to receive prospecting letters. I use the computer to "undupe" these names against all prospect lists because I want to treat these people as special. I want to treat these folks like I know them, as friends. I also want to sell these customers higher-end products. I want to up-sell these folks.

But this rule likely only applies to the top 20 percent or 30 percent of the best buyers on my customer list. The rest of your house list (the bottom 70 percent or so) can and should continue to receive prospecting offers—that is, you can treat them as though they are not on your house list. So don't "undupe" these names against prospecting lists.

"Undupe" is slang that means eliminate duplicates between the lists you are mailing.

Your "house list" is a somewhat elastic term.

For the purpose of this discussion, I define it as those who have bought something within the last 12 months. After that, they are treated as prospect names.

The reasons for not "unduping" the bottom 70 or even 80 percent of your house list against the prospect lists you are mailing are many. But here are three key reasons for making sure these weaker buyers are not omitted ("unduped") from your prospect mailings:

1) **You want to identify your repeat buyers as quickly as possible because your multi-buyers are at least three times more likely to buy again than those who have not bought again from you.**

   Many on your house list will respond with a purchase to a prospect package. Some will respond only to prospect offers, and don't care much about personalized offers and don't respond to "up-selling." Buyers are not very valuable to your business until they become repeat buyers.

2) **You know only one thing for certain about customers who have bought only once from you.**

   They liked that offer. So do your level best to keep sending them more of the same. If they like Coca-Cola, keep selling them more Coca-Cola. Don't keep trying to sell them chocolate milk if they keep declining this offer.

3) "Repeat, repeat, repeat" your message is a key marketing principle.

Nike, McDonalds, Crest, Tide, and the most successful consumer brands show the same ads over and over again because they know it will take many impressions on your brain before their message sinks in. The same is true in direct mail, which is just another form of advertising. Your message must be simple, focused, and repeated over and over again to your target market. Just because they answered your letter once does not mean they remember answering it. Nor does it mean they could explain to their friends what you do, what your product is, or even what your company is named.

Most people answer direct mail offers out of impulse.

They liked what they read at that moment. They ordered the product and then went on to something else. A few days later, they've forgotten your letter and your company completely. They probably will forget they even ordered your product until they receive it.

The big advertisers know this fact of life. They know they can't stop repeating their message to their target audience. They know the battle for market share is really a battle for a share of people's attention, a battle for minds. That's why you should continue mailing a successful prospect package until it stops working. It's also why you should not "undupe" your house list against prospect lists, except for the best 20 percent or 30 percent of your customers who clearly do know about you and your company and should be treated with extra care.

I would say there are very few good reasons to prevent the bottom 70 percent of your house list from receiving prospecting letters. In fact, not keeping these names in your prospect mailings can be catastrophic to both your house list and prospecting mail programs.

And the reason is this...

Unduping your entire house list against prospect lists can cut your prospect results in half if you have a large housefile of 100,000 buyers or more. Someone must pay for prospect losses (the continued building of your house list). It might as well be the weaker names on your house list who help pay for your customer-acquisition program.

Unduping your entire house list against prospect lists will also hurt your house list offers by failing to deliver more prospect mail to your one-time buyers, which, in turn, will give them fewer opportunities to become multi-buyers.

Your prospect "customer acquisition letters" letters are usually your least expensive packages, because they're produced in large quantities. Making sure your weaker customers receive prospect mail is a great way to keep your company's name or your brand name in front of your lukewarm buyers. And you're achieving this goal with low-cost packages that have proven to be successful.

7. Protect your list.

Your housefile list is your most valuable asset. Protect it by salting your list with about fifty decoy or seed names. These are names and addresses scattered throughout your housefile of people who are not real customers but are monitoring all mailings to your list.

You'll want to include these decoy names whenever you rent or exchange your list and whenever you mail a letter to your list. Your decoy names should have addresses representing every geographic region of the country or area to which you are mailing. The best decoy names are friends and relatives you have scattered across the country. Ask your decoys to be diligent about sending you every letter they receive as part of your own housefile program or others mailing to your housefile as part of a name-exchange or list rental arrangement.

Your decoy names should use fictitious first names or fictitious middle initials to distinguish mailings to your housefile from their other mail. And your decoy helpers should write the date on the outer envelopes they receive showing when the letter arrived before mailing your "seed" letters back to you.

In addition, there are companies that specialize in list security and can provide unique decoy names for salting your list. One company is called U.S. Monitor. There are others as well. Your decoys should respond to some offers and develop a buying history so they will be treated as real customers.

There are many reasons why you should take such elaborate measures with your system of decoy names to track all mailings to your housefile:

1) **You'll know immediately if your housefile has been stolen and is being used for unauthorized mailings.**

   Your list is protected under trade and copyright laws as private property. But the law requires you to show that you have taken reasonable steps to protect your list. And you must be able to demonstrate with your decoys that your list has been stolen and is being used for unauthorized mailings. Courts recognize a decoy system as strong evidence of illegal use of your mailing list.

2) **You'll want to track when your own mailings arrive in people's homes.**

   If all your decoys receive your mailing on schedule, you'll know there was no production problem with your mailing. Unfortunately, mailshops sometimes mess up and fail to get mailings out on time. Your decoy system will alert you to any problems with your mailing.

3) **If you're renting your list to others for a one-time use, your decoy system will let you know your renters are mailing your list only once, are mailing on schedule, and are mailing the letter you approved.**

   Think of your house list as a safe full of money. Don't leave your safe open for anyone to walk in and take what they please.

If your list is of any significant size, anyone with even a modest knowledge of direct marketing could easily take your list if it's not protected and make hundreds of thousands or even millions of dollars with it. Even if they never mailed to it themselves, they could make an enormous sum of money just renting your list under a different name, perhaps as part of a compilation list along with other lists they might have.

Most people I have run into in this business are very honest. But there are professional list thieves out there who understand very well the value of a mailing list. Theft of your list could severely damage or even destroy your business.

8. Keep an updated copy of your housefile in a safe deposit box.

Once a week or so, put a complete and updated copy of your house list in a safe deposit box. Fires and other accidents happen. Computers crash.

Sometimes sabotage occurs. You always want to keep an updated copy of your housefile in a safe deposit box at a bank. This is your back-up plan that can protect you from disaster.

You have invested a lot of money to build your house list. Take every step to protect it. Guard it like Fort Knox.

Chapter Seventy-Eight
Your checklist of vital direct mail basics

No airline pilot would think of taking off without running through a regular checklist. Nor should you mail any direct mail marketing package without always and religiously going through this list of critical direct mail basics.

You know what happens when you "ASSUME." That's right, you make an ASS out of U and ME. Most important, you risk making a catastrophically costly blunder.

You should make sure your graphic artist, your production department and everyone involved with your mailings have a copy of this checklist of VITAL DIRECT MAIL BASICS:

1. Be sure to say who to write the check to clearly and prominently on the order form.

I know this seems so simple and obvious, but I've seen direct mail packages that fail to say prominently, or even mention at all, to whom to write out the check. I often have to scour the offer for quite a while before I discover (or guess) from the fine print what company name I should write on the check.

2. Put your company name and address, the Web site address and the 1.800 number on all major components, except perhaps the outer envelope.

You want to build some name recognition. Also, quite a few people (about six percent) will use their own envelopes to send their payments, perhaps because they've lost the reply envelope you've sent them. Always make it as easy as possible for people to order.

So it's very important to put the name and address of the company on every component in the package. As a general rule, I don't put the company's name on the carrier envelope, because it tells the reader that this is probably a sales pitch. I usually like to create mystery on the carrier. But you should include the name and address of the company— where to send the check—on all other items in the package.

3. Put footers in the bottom right corner of each page directing your reader to keep reading.

Footers on letters should say (Please continue letter), (Over, please), (Next page, please) or some phrase to let the reader know there is more to read.

4. Number the pages.

Though there's no need to number the first page. I like to spell out page numbers—Page Two, Page Three, etc. This makes the letter look more personal and high end.

5. Try not to end a page with a period.

Have the sentence break in the middle and continue on to the next page, if at all possible. Strive to have this be an especially interesting sentence that will compel your reader to turn to the next page and keep reading.

6. Use an old-fashioned typewriter font for your letter to consumers.

For your consumer letters, Courier and Prestige are the best fonts for your letter. Avoid using a desktop publishing font like Helvetica or Times Roman on the letter. It's okay to use a desktop publishing font such as Times Roman for your business-to-business sales letters.

In your packages to consumers, you may use desktop publishing fonts with your enclosures and inserts, anything that's not the letter, which should look like it's been typed (even though everyone will know you used a computer). You should periodically conduct a font test to see if more orders continue to come in with Courier than with a desktop publishing font like Times Roman. Courier is still winning the tests I've conducted lately.

The old typewriter-look still just looks more personal and friendly.

This rule no longer applies to business-to-business letters. Business executives today expect the more boring, vanilla, Times Roman font in letters from other business executives.

7. Indent the first lines in paragraphs of letters five spaces.

Indents are a device to catch the eye of your reader and keep your reader moving through your letter.

8. Paragraphs should not be more than six lines.

Big blocks of undifferentiated text are intimidating to readers. They're also ugly.

Long paragraphs and large blocks of text just look like too much work to wade through. Your letters must be scannable, eye catching, and easy to read. Don't make every paragraph the same length. Some paragraphs can be just a few words, or even just one word. Others can be one line, two lines, or three lines. Mix it up, but no paragraph should be more than six lines.

9. The signature should be in blue ink.

The signature should look as real as possible and should stand out.

Black signatures blend in too much with the rest of the black letter copy. People expect signatures to be blue, not green, red, orange, pink, or some other color. Also, be sure the signature is legible, not one of those doctor's signatures you can't read.

For high-end customers, consider actually hand-signing each letter. It's obvious to readers when a signature is real, not printed. So it may well be worth actually hand signing letters to your best customers. It doesn't take long to hand sign a thousand letters.

I've also found inks that will smudge a bit after they are printed, further enhancing the personal look of printed signatures. The signature and how it looks are important.

Most readers will look at the signature area first to see who the letter is from.

10. To draw special attention to a particular paragraph, indent every line in the paragraph ten spaces (one inch) on both sides.

This is just another way to enhance the "scannability" of your letter. For these special block-style extra-indented paragraphs, you can bend the *no paragraphs longer than six lines rule* a bit.

11. Lines in letters should be single spaced with one additional space separating paragraphs.

Again, readability, ease on the eyes, and "scannability" are what you are striving for with your layout. This is just how letters should look.

12. Do not justify the right margin of letters.

The right margin of your letter should be ragged. Not only does a justified right margin make for more difficult reading, it destroys the personal look of your letter.

I once had a printer present me with the final printed copy of my letter, boasting with a smile that he had "fixed it" by justifying the right margin. He thought I would be pleased with his diligence. More than 500,000 copies had been printed.

Aaarrrrrrgh!

How To Write...

13. Be sure all photos and exhibits include a caption or note of explanation.

A direct mail marketing letter, a sales letter, is like a show-and-tell-presentation. Always explain to your readers what you are showing them.

If you are enclosing a photo, a newspaper article or other exhibit, these must include notes of explanations. I often like blue or red handwritten notes. If you are enclosing an article on the company's product or service, yellow highlighting works well to draw the reader's attention to key points, especially when combined with handwritten notes in the margin.

14. Shorten the name of the letter signer to sound more familiar and friendly.

Instead of "Louis" use "Lou." Instead of "Benjamin" use "Ben." Instead of "Katherine" use "Kathy." The exception to this rule is if the letter is signed by a general, a judge, or some other very high government official. In these cases, using a shortened first name or nickname could weaken the power of the official title.

"General Robert E. Lee" is far stronger and more appropriate than "General Bob Lee."

But for the typical head of a business, it's better to use the more familiar sounding shortened first name. Congressmen and senators should also use the shortened version of their names in their letters. "Congressman Tom Delay" is far better than "Congressman Thomas Delay."

15. Put in place a proofreading system.

Each page should be initialed by two people who have read every word of the package carefully. This will minimize mistakes. The reality is that a typo will not usually depress the results of a mailing, but it can be embarrassing.

16. "First Class" should be stamped in red twice on reply envelopes if they are not BREs.

This helps draw the reader's attention to the reply envelope, emphasizes urgency, and suggests that a reply is expected.

The exception to this rule is if you are using a large commercial first-class envelope with a green diamond border or some other special reply envelope that is heavy on graphics, such as a FedEx or UPS envelope.

17. First-class mail should look first class.

Don't use fuzzy ink jets or crummy-looking Cheshire labels on your reply forms for first-class mail. You're spending a lot of money to mail your letter first class. Make everything in your letter look personal. Your first-class letter should look like a letter from a close friend.

18. Put more than one stamp on first-class mail.

This helps emphasize that this is first-class mail and also helps make the letter look more personal.

If you're paying for first-class mail, make sure the donor will notice it. I like putting eight stamps on envelopes. This helps create interest. It's like a neon sign telling the recipient of the letter, "Look at me, this is a first-class letter."

19. Don't put mail codes or other ugly numbers near the reader's name or other personalized message.

This completely destroys the personal effect your packages are attempting to achieve. No one wants to be treated like a number.

20. On every reply form should appear this instruction: *"Please make any necessary corrections to your name and address on this reply form."*

This should appear in red right under the reader's address. Failure to be a fanatic about correcting and updating your customer list is one of the surest ways to go out of business. Be a nut-case about the accuracy and cleanliness of your customer list.

21. Determine your defaults for personalization.

The defaults might be different for the address and salutation parts of the letter than for the body of the letter (and probably will be). In general,

How To Write...

your first choice in your salutation should be: "Dear [Title/last name]." If you don't have your reader's title in the title field of your database, then just use [First Name only]. If no name is available, use [Dear Friend] or nothing if personalization is asked for in the body of letter.

The unfortunate reality is that no database is perfect. Every database is missing information. Your default strategy must account for missing information. So think through all the personalization defaults for each part of the letter where personalization is called for. You're paying a lot for personalization. Make sure it's done right and that you make the most of it. Again, wrong personalization will do more harm than no personalization.

22. Look for opportunities to personalize.

I see a lot of money spent on personalization, and then opportunities are missed for personalization. Refer in your letter to the donor's town and state, past purchases, and other information collected as part of the customer's record in your computer database.

23. Take every step to make your personal letter look and feel personal.

Laser the reader's name and address above the salutation on the letter. Put a specific date on the letter, as you would if writing a personal letter to a business associate. If you are personalizing every page of the letter, as you might in a letter to your best clients and customers when sending a major proposal, put the person's title and full name stacked over the page number in the upper right corner of each page.

However, don't overuse the reader's name in the body of the letter. This can look phony and insincere. When writing to a friend, you would never use your friend's name throughout the body of the letter. This is fake personalization and destroys the genuine personal and serious effect you are striving for.

24. Get on every mailing list you can.

Answer your junk mail with orders, especially if you are impressed with the offer and the mailing. If you see the same package coming through your mailbox over and over again, you know it's a winner. Borrow the idea for your own mailings (obviously not word for word).

25. Put list "source codes" on all order and reply forms.

Be sure to include codes on reply forms identifying the list or house list segment the order or response came in from. You'll need this information to track the results of your mailings. I might break a house list mailing into 10, 20, or more segments, each with its own code. This will allow me to track how each segment is performing and whether I should drop or add some segments to future house list mailings.

Similarly, each prospect list will also require its own code on the response form so you can track how each list is performing. You can't produce reports on mailings or track the results without source-coding your reply forms. Putting list *source codes* on all reply forms is absolutely fundamental to managing every aspect of your direct mail program.

26. Make list "source codes" a permanent part of a customer's history in your database.

Every order must be linked to a source code. This information will allow you not only to track how particular lists and list segments are performing, but will allow you to tailor future offers to what your customers actually want. Source codes (sometimes called "motivation codes") allow you to target buyers and groups of buyers with laser-like precision and maximize your profit.

27. Bid out all jobs.

Don't use the same printer and mailshop all the time. You'll find they will start becoming complacent about the work and your prices will start slowly creeping up. Bid out every job. And once the lowest bid comes back, offer additional incentives to get the price lower. One incentive I use is the likelihood of future big rollouts if this is a prospect package. The cost of the package is often the difference between a success and failure for a mailing.

28. Cut costs by projecting your needs into the future.

Take advantage of downtimes (bad mail times) for your vendors to get lower costs and then mail later. Also, if you know you are going to mail 300,000 copies of the same prospect package or offer each month, consider printing 600,000 and hold half in inventory until the next mail date. Obviously, this approach only works for the very big mailers.

29. Use low-grade paper and consider reducing paper weight.

You buy paper by the pound. So, for your lower-end offers ask your printer if it's cheaper to print on 50-pound instead of the more typical 60-pound paper. You'll want to test this to see if the more flimsy paper hurts your results. I have not seen any difference for my prospect and low-end offers. However, you'll probably want to use heavier, more impressive paper for your best customers.

30. Become familiar with how your printers and mailshops work most efficiently.

Ask your printer and mailshop for suggestions on how to cut the cost of your package without compromising the look and feel of your offer. For example, your vendor's ability to laser letters on continuous forms will help you economize. Some printers can personalize all four pages on one big sheet of paper and have a machine slice and fold the paper all at once, thus avoiding the problem and cost of a four-way letter match.

Good direct mail copywriters and creative people thoroughly understand the capabilities of the vendors they are using. Ask your vendors for copies of all the formats they offer. Treat your vendors like the partners they are. Describe what you are trying to do and the impact you want to achieve. Ask for samples of the largest volume mailings they've produced over the last six months. Your printers and mailshops will be happy to give you all kinds of ideas if you ask and bring them into the creative process early.

31. Don't use bleeds in your artwork if you don't have to.

A bleed is running the color to the edge of the paper. This is expensive. It's hard to imagine an instance when this extra cost is really necessary for your direct mail marketing offer. In fact, fancy, slick-looking graphic art usually depresses returns.

32. Don't use graphic art that makes your printer's job more difficult than necessary.

Avoid creating a graphic design that requires a lot of careful, detailed work by the printer. You'll just run up your cost without improving returns. Beauty is not what you are trying to achieve with your graphic art. Graphic art's role is to enhance the communication of your message. Simple headlines are the main job of the graphic artist.

33. Don't print deadline dates.

Deadline dates should be handled by lasers and inkjets—not a printing press. You'll want the freedom to adjust any deadline dates you have in the package. Mail dates are missed all the time for all kinds of reasons. You don't want your mailing to go out after the deadline or "due back by" date in the letter or on the reply form. And if you have inventory, you'll want the freedom to change the deadline date so you can use the inventory later.

34. Plan in advance.

Few things are more costly than rushing a job and making last-minute changes.

Sometimes rush jobs can't be avoided, especially in political campaigns and issue fundraising. But 98 percent of rush jobs I see are the result of poor planning. Do a mock-up or dummy of your package to make sure it all fits together, especially if your package uses odd-size envelopes.

For example, make sure your reply form fits neatly and easily in the reply envelope. Have your package checked in advance by the post office (before you print and insert) to make sure you're in compliance with postal regulations and get all the bulk mail discounts you're expecting.

35. Check all bills carefully.

A surprisingly high percentage of bills that come in from your direct mail program will be incorrect. And very few of these incorrect bills will be lower than you expect. They will be higher. Be sure to

How To Write...

compare your bills to all your signed purchase orders. In fact, make sure all orders are done with a written purchase order. Order nothing verbally.

36. Decide the insertion order of components.

The insertion order makes a difference in results of the package. Typically you'll want your letter to be the first item your reader sees. But sometimes you'll use a special attention-getting device (such as a $1 bill, free gift, or USPS priority mail reply envelope). In this case, you'll want the attention-getting device to how first, since the purpose of the attention-getting device is to get the reader's attention.

Whatever the insertion order of your package, make sure it's a conscious decision. Determining the insertion order of components is part of your marketing strategy. Nothing should be left up to the mailshop to decide. Nothing should be left to chance.

37. Require the mailshop to provide you with a "live" sample of your package before it mails.

And when I say "live," I mean not a sample or a mock-up.

I mean an actual copy of the package that is going to a real person with postage affixed. Once you've seen the package, held it, and inspected it, you can then go down to the mailbox and mail it yourself.

38. Be sure you are one of the people on the list receiving the mailing.

You will want to see what your package looks like after it's been sent through the mail stream. After the post office gets done with your package, it might look like a truck has run over it. Your package was beautiful, worthy of display at the Smithsonian Museum of Art when it was at the mailshop. But now it's barely recognizable, looks awful.

There's nothing you can do about the post office mangling your mailing. I have found that I often need to put the mailing in a more durable, industrial-looking carrier.

The point is, your mailing might look very different after the post office has finished running it through its machines, throwing it, stomping on it, stuffing it in a tiny mail box, and whatever else the post office does with it.

Also, mailshops make mistakes all the time. They put the wrong letter in packages. They forget to include the reply envelope. There's almost no limit to the kinds of incredible mistakes I've seen made by mailshops. Every time I think I've seen just about every error that can be made, a new one hits me in the face, a mistake I never could have thought of or imagined happening. The only way you might ever know about a major mistake made on your mailing is if you are on the list being mailed.

In fact, you will want to have at least a dozen decoy names on your list, not just to make sure your list has not been stolen as discussed earlier, but also so you will see what your mailing looks like when it arrives in mailboxes.

Chapter Seventy-Nine
Six of the greatest sales letters of all time

I reprint here six of the greatest sales letters ever written.

They are great not because of their eloquence. They are great not because I think they are great. They are great for one reason and one reason alone. They are great because these letters, combined, have generated billions of dollars in sales.

These letters are successful because these letter writers understand exactly what people want and specifically what their readers are looking for.

Sales letter writing is a specialized genre, involving the science of persuasion. And it is a science, with established laws and rules that can be learned by anyone who is willing to take the time and expend the effort.

The easiest, fastest way to learn a skill is to study the best.

These letters follow a proven set of rules that all sales letters must follow to be successful. If you study these letters and learn these rules, your sales letters will improve dramatically. These letters (some of them written a half century ago) will also demonstrate why the well-executed letter is still, by far, the most powerful sales tool. Read these letters again and again. Here they are.

The Wall Street Journal
The Daily Diary of the American Dream

22 Cortlandt Street/New York, New York 10007

Dear Reader:

On a beautiful late spring afternoon, twenty-five years ago, two young men graduated from the same college. They were very much alike, these two young men.

Both had been better than average students, both were personable and both -- as young college graduates are -- were filled with ambitious dreams for the future.

Recently, these men returned to their college for their 25th reunion.

They were still very much alike.

Both were happily married. Both had three children. And both, it turned out, had gone to work for the same Midwestern manufacturing company after graduation, and were still there.

But there was a difference. One of the men was manager of a small department of that company. The other was its president.

What Made The Difference

Have you ever wondered, as I have, what makes this kind of difference in people's lives? It isn't always a native intelligence or talent or dedication. It isn't that one person wants success and the other doesn't.

The difference lies in what each person knows and how he or she makes use of that knowledge.

And that is why I am writing to you and to people like you about The Wall Street Journal. For that is the whole purpose of The Journal: To give its readers knowledge - knowledge that they can use in business.

A Publication Unlike Any Other

You see, The Wall Street Journal is a unique publication. It's the country's only national business daily. Each business day, it is put together by the world's largest staff of business news experts.

Each business day, The Journal's pages include a broad range of information of interest and significance to business-minded people, no matter where it comes from. Not just stocks and finance, but anything and everything in the whole, fast-moving world of business...The Wall Street Journal gives you all the business news you need -- when you need it.

Knowledge Is Power

Right now, I am reading page one of The Journal. It combines all the important news of the day with in-depth feature reporting. Every phase of business news is covered, from articles on inflation, wholesale prices, car prices, tax incentives for industries to major developments in Washington, and elsewhere.

And there is page after page inside The Journal filled with fascinating and significant information that's useful to you. A daily column on personal money management helps you become a smarter saver, better investor, wiser spender. There are weekly columns on small business, marketing, real estate, technology, regional developments. If you have never read The Wall Street Journal, you cannot imagine how useful it can be to you.

Much of the information that appears in The Journal appears nowhere else. The Journal is printed in numerous plants across the United States, so that you get it early each business day.

A $28 Subscription

Put our statements to the proof by subscribing for the next 13 weeks for just $28. This is the shortest subscription term we offer -- and a perfect way to get acquainted with The Journal.

Or you may prefer to take advantage of a longer-term subscription for greater savings: an annual subscription at $107 saves you $20 off The Journal's cover price. Our best buy -- two years for $185 -- saves you a full $69!

Simply fill out the endorsed order card and mail it in the postage-paid envelope provided. And here's The Journal guarantee: Should The Journal not measure up to your expectations, you may cancel this trial arrangement at any point and receive a refund for the undelivered portion of your subscription.

If you feel as we do that this is a fair and reasonable proposition, then you will want to find out without delay if The Wall Street Journal can do for you what it is doing for millions of readers. So please mail the enclosed order card now, and we will start serving you immediately.

About those two college classmates, I mention at the beginning of this letter. They graduated from college together and together got started in the business world. So what made their lives in business different?

Knowledge. Useful knowledge. And its application.

An Investment In Success

I cannot promise you that success will be

```
instantly yours if you start reading The Wall
Street Journal. But I can guarantee that you will
find The Journal always interesting, always
reliable, and always useful.

                    Sincerely Yours,


                    Peter R. Kann
                    Executive Vice President/
                    Associate Publisher

PRK:vb
Enc:

P.S. It's important to note that The Journal's
     subscription price may be tax-deductible.
```

This is the legendary "two young men" letter that *The Wall Street Journal* used for decades to build its circulation.

You've probably received many versions of this in your mailbox over the years.

The letter makes its point by starting with a brief, but compelling story about the fortunes of two young men who have similar educations and backgrounds. Interestingly, the letter does not claim that the more successful young man was a reader of the *Journal*.

But the story is an attention-getter.

A brief, compelling story that illustrates your point is one of the most powerful sales techniques because you are telling by showing. Aesop's fables are far more powerful than simply telling a child the rules of morality.

Jesus taught by using parables. He knew that a story would have far more impact on His audience than simply telling us how to act and how to think.

In fact, almost the entire Bible is stories. Yes, we're also given the Ten Commandments, the Sermon on the Mount and Paul's Epistles—in case we missed the point of the stories. But more than 90 percent of the Bible is stories. Most of us can't recite all Ten Commandments. But we all remember the stories.

The Bible is the best selling book of all time. So stories clearly work.

How To Write...

Can you think of ways to use brief but compelling stories to strengthen your sales letters and presentations?

Notice, also, that This *Wall Street Journal* letter includes a strong offer and a guarantee—mandatory features of every successful mass-market sales letter to consumers. Study the "two young men" letter carefully. Your sales letters will improve significantly and immediately.

$$* * * *$$

Now examine closely each and every sentence of this amazing letter *Newsweek* used for decades to build its circulation. As you read, ask yourself, what is the purpose of this sentence? Why did the writer choose this word? Because every sentence and every word in this letter has a definite purpose. This is a truly brilliantly constructed sales letter.

Newsweek
117 East Third Street
Dayton, Ohio 45402

Dear Reader:

   If the list upon which I found your name is any indication, this is not the first -- nor will it be the last -- subscription letter you receive.

   Quite frankly, your education and income set you apart from the general population and make you a highly rated prospect for everything from magazines to mutual funds.

   You've undoubtedly "heard everything" by now in the way of promises and premiums. I won't try to top any of them.

   Nor will I insult your intelligence.

   If you subscribe to Newsweek, you won't get rich quick. You won't bowl over friends and business associates with clever remarks and sage comments after your first copy of Newsweek arrives. (Your conversation will benefit from a better understanding of the events and forces of our era, but that's all. Wit and wisdom are gifts no magazine can bestow.) And should you attain further professional or business success during the term of your subscription, you'll have your own native ability and good luck to thank for it -- not Newsweek.

What, then, can Newsweek do for you?

The answer depends upon what type of person you happen to be.

If you are not curious about what's going on outside your own immediate daily range of concern... if you are quickly bored when the topic of conversation shifts from your house, your car, your ambitions... if you couldn't care less about what's happening in Washington or Wall Street, in London or Moscow... then forget Newsweek. It can't do a thing for you.

If, on the other hand, you are the kind of individual who would like to keep up with national and international affairs, space and nuclear science, the arts -- but cannot spend hours at it...if you're genuinely interested in what's going on with other members of the human race...if you recognize the big stake you have in decisions made in Washington and Wall Street, in London and in Moscow...

then Newsweek may well be the smartest small investment you could make for the weeks ahead.

For just 11 cents a week, as a Newsweek subscriber, your interest in national and international affairs will be served by over 200 top-notch reporters here and around the world. Each week, you'll read the most significant facts taken from their daily dispatches by Newsweek's editors.

How To Write...

You'll get the facts. No bias. No slanting.
We respect your right to form your own
opinion.

In the eventful political arena, in weeks to come,
you'll read about...

JOHNSON - How will government spending for the
          Great Society programs affect the
          nation's economy?

FOREIGN
POLICY - What settlement is possible in Vietnam?
         What role for the Buddhists, the army,
         the Viet Cong?

THE
ISSUES - Our stance toward Red China. Domestic
         crises in civil rights, in education,
         the war on poverty! What solutions are
         best?

You'll stay abreast of events on the world scene
as the Kremlin bosses cope with unrest in the
satellite nations and with Peking's bid to dominate
Red affairs...as Western Europe develops new
economic ties and increasingly competes in world
markets...and as chaos and unrest seethe up in
Africa and Southeast Asia.

You'll also keep on top of latest developments
in the exciting fields of space and nuclear
science. Whether the story describes a manned
space probe of the Moon or the opening of a new
chapter in peaceful uses of atomic fission, you'll
learn the key facts -- in plain English -- from
Newsweek's regular department of Science and Space.

The fascinating world of art will be reviewed
and previewed for you in Newsweek. Whether you're
interested in books or ballet, painting or plays,
movies or music -- or all of them -- you will find
it covered fully and fairly in Newsweek.

Subscribe now and you'll read about

International film awards...controversial art shows at New York's Museum of Modern Art or the great galleries of Europe...triumphant concert tours by famed virtuosos...glittering first nights on and off Broadway...plus revealing interviews with colorful personalities -- authors, prima donnas, actors, musicians.

AND you'll be briefed on happenings in the worlds of business and finance (What's ahead now for steel output, auto sales? How will the market react?) ...Education and Religion (More "machine" teaching? Closer interfaith cooperation?)...Science and Medicine (New breakthroughs in cancer and arthritis research?)...Sports and TV-Radio (New higher standards, less violence in both?)

TRY Newsweek.

Try it now at this special introductory rate:

27 WEEKS OF NEWSWEEK FOR ONLY $2.97

That's just 11 cents a week -- a little more than a penny-and-a-half a day!

And try it with this guarantee: if, after examining several issues in your own home, you do not agree that Newsweek satisfies your news interests, you'll receive a prompt refund on unmailed copies.

An order form is enclosed, along with a postage-paid return envelope.

Do initial and return the order form today. We'll bill you later if you wish.

Sincerely,

S. Arthur Dembner
Circulation Director

How To Write...

I'm almost certain (though not 100%) that this letter was written by the great copywriter Ed McLean, who wrote many of *Newsweek's* sales letters. For decades, this letter powered the explosive growth of Newsweek's circulation, making *Newsweek* a serious competitor to *Time*.

Here are four elements that make this letter great:

1) Straight-forward honesty

The letter begins by telling the reader what *Newsweek* is not, and what *Newsweek* won't do for the reader.

This is the classic "start-with-a-damaging-admission" strategy. This builds credibility for the rest of the letter. *Newsweek* won't make you rich, won't help you advance your career, and won't impress your friends.

The letter then goes into all the interesting topics and issues covered by the magazine. But the letter would not have been nearly as strong if it had started with this catalogue of what you'll find in the magazine. Starting with a damaging admission not only builds credibility for the rest of the letter in the mind of the reader, it's also just more interesting to read about weaknesses than strengths.

No one wants to listen to a braggart. But ears will perk up if you begin by clearly describing what you cannot do.

In addition, starting a letter by listing weaknesses is one of the best ways to instantly communicate your USP—your Unique Selling Proposition.

2) Casual, conversational, engaging style

This letter sounds a lot like someone having a casual conversation with the reader. It's breezy, filled with interesting details and provocative questions. There's nothing pedantic in this letter. A fourth grader could easily read and understand it.

3) Understated formatting

This letter contains none of the screaming headlines that we see in most direct mail solicitations. This helps reinforce the letter's credibility. It just doesn't look like all the other junk mail we receive. It looks like a real letter, even though it's not personalized (to save on cost).

...Blockbuster Sales Letters   197

But the writer does use a number of understated formatting tricks to catch the reader's eye. You'll see some ellipses as well as some unusual indents. Some paragraphs are indented; while others are not. Indeed, some of the formatting almost looks like it was a mistake, which is eye-catching in itself—but you can be certain it was all intentional, aimed at catching the reader's eye and making the letter easily scannable.

4) Strong offer

For a penny-and-a-half a day, you can try *Newsweek*. And if you don't like the magazine, you can receive a full refund for any unmailed copies.

Nothing very unusual here. This is the type of offer you'll see in many successful direct mail sales letters. But the casual way in which the letter communicates the offer and the guarantee also helps establish credibility. The letter uses no intelligence-insulting "hype" words such as "greatest" or "best ever" that you see in so many sales pitches. Just the facts. Here's the offer—"take it or leave it" is the impression the letter leaves with the reader. We'd love to have you as a subscriber, but we're not desperate either. And we're certainly not going to sell you hard by overstating what we are. What I'm describing is exactly what you'll get.

Wouldn't it be great if every advertiser took this approach? We might then actually pay attention to the ads. Every sales letter and advertising copywriter would do well simply by imitating the approach of this letter.

* * * *

Here's another terrific letter, this one from *Popular Mechanics*—the language and tone calibrated perfectly for the rugged, roll-up-your sleeves, jack-of-all-trades, handy-man-type fellow this letter is trying to reach.

How To Write...

Popular Mechanics

250 WEST 55TH STREET, NEW YORK, N.Y. 10019

```
*************************************
```
If you want to <u>live better</u>...

<u>Don't mind</u> hard work...

<u>Like to pay your own way...</u>

<u>Let me ship you VOL. I of the exciting</u>
POPULAR MECHANICS DO-IT-YOURSELF
ENCYCLOPEDIA.

And I want you to <u>keep</u> it. FREE!

```
*************************************
```

Good Friend,

This invitation isn't for deadbeats, rip-off
artists or "gentlemen" who hate to get their hands
dirty.

It's for the rest of us.

It's for the average guy who works hard for a
living (and wants to live better). Who knows the
value of a buck (about 50 cents these days.) Who is
willing to trade a few drops of sweat for the
chance to save big bucks.

It's for guys who aren't afraid to get down
under the sink with a pipe wrench. Guys who don't
mind sticking their hands in the toilet tank to
adjust a ball cock (because they know it's going to
save a $16 plumber's bill).

Our country was built on the sweat and
hard work of <u>do-it-yourself</u> guys. And

from POPULAR MECHANICS, the #1 do-it-yourself magazine, we'd just like to say THANK YOU.

Our big, illustrated POPULAR MECHANICS DO-IT-YOURSELF ENCYCLOPEDIA was written with "shirtsleeves" guys in mind. Guys <u>like you</u>.

So please -- let me ship you Volume I FREE. (<u>No</u> strings attached. <u>No purchase</u> necessary.)

It's BIG -- 168 oversized pages crammed with up-to-date money-saving plans, photos, diagrams and articles about how-to-do-just about EVERYTHING!

From fixing your car's alternator to improving your gas mileage by 30 percent!

From drilling an angled hole accurately, to resurfacing your asphalt driveway or fixing a small appliance.

It's PRACTICAL -- oversized pages lay down flat so you have them right there on your shop table or car fender to refer to. Sturdy hard-covers laugh at dirt!

Type is LARGE so it's easy-to-read.

Each article is generously illustrated -- Volume I alone has more then 600 step-by-step drawings, photos and diagrams.

SPEAKING OF SAVING, HAVE YOU BEEN TO A BODY SHOP LATELY? If it was within the past 12 months, you know the cost of auto body repairs has zoomed out of sight!

So we got the manger of a big body shop near our office to share his trade secrets with us. The results? An article illustrated with how-to-do-it photos that shows you how to get rid of scratches, dents, rust and rotten spots yourself -- make your fender look like new!

How To Write...

All this, and much more, is in Volume I of the POPULAR MECHANICS DO-IT-YOURSELF ENCYCLOPEDIA.

But remember -- you don't pay a cent for it. Now or ever. And there's no obligation -- NO PURCHASES NECESSARY!

"Well, come on," you're probably saying, "There's gotta be a catch."

MAYBE THERE IS.

Sure, I'd like to sell you the whole POPULAR MECHANICS DO-IT-YOURSELF ENCYCLOPEDIA.

But I know from experience that I can't "sell" someone like you. You've got to prove for yourself it's worthwhile. So accept our FREE book and examine Volume I, then make up your own mind.

> VOLUME I IS YOUR FREE SAMPLE. AND I WANT YOU
> TO USE IT FOR ALL IT'S WORTH.

Got kids? Turn to page 50 for complete plans and instructions for making your own hockey tabletop game. (You'll have a ball with it too.) It would cost you plenty in a store. But you can make it with a few dollars worth of lumber, particleboard, and an old range exhaust fan.

Want a greenhouse? On pages 30-32 you'll find plans for an elegant addition -- an add-on Greenhouse.

How about valuable antiques? Why not build your own authentic reproduction pine and maple bench... for a fraction of what an original would cost. Complete plans and instructions start on Page 30.

Turn to page 178 to see how easy it is to do all your own routine auto service and maintenance. (If you're spending $200 a year to have a pro do it, you could save $150!)

Cool your house in the summer (and cut your air conditioning electric bills) by installing an attic fan. The article starting on page 156 shows you how.

I could go on and on. But why should I? Volume I of POPULAR MECHANICS DO-IT-YOURSELF ENCYCLOPEDIA is yours for the asking.

You don't even pay to send for it. Postage paid Reply Card enclosed.

So what are you waiting for? Say YES today!

When your "Free sample" arrives, keep it. And use it. And see for yourself why POPULAR MECHANICS is usually considered the world's leading source of "do-it-yourself" information.

NOW LISTEN TO THIS.

If Volume I isn't everything I've promised, just drop us a note saying "No more!" That will be the end of it (of course, you keep Volume I).

But if you are pleased as I expect, just sit back and enjoy your Free Volume. Then, eight weeks later, you'll receive Volume II of the POPULAR MECHANICS DO-IT-YOURSELF ENCYCLOPEDIA -- Just as big, beautiful, husky and crammed with plans and information as the first one. For example:

HOW TO TEST & RECHARGE MOST BATTERIES...BUILD YOUR OWN BARBECUE BAR...FINISH YOUR BASEMENT LIKE A PRO...PUT IN A STAIRWELL...INSTALL A HALF-BATH ANYWHERE. PLUS EVERYTHING YOU OUGHT TO KNOW ABOUT HANDSAWS...HOW TO REMOVE A BEARING WALL...ALL ABOUT BELT SANDERS...CHOOSING THE RIGHT BIKE...AND MUCH, MUCH MORE!

That's just a sample of Volume II. But remember -- YOU HAVEN'T YET SPENT OR RISKED A PENNY:

Because Volume II is yours to examine and use freely for 14 days: Then, if you are not completely "sold" on the POPULAR MECHANICS DO-IT-YOURSELF ENCYCLOPEDIA, just return it before the Free-Examination Period is over, and owe <u>nothing</u>.

By now, however, if you're the kind of guy I think you are, you should be itching to get your hands on the remaining 18 volumes of the POPULAR MECHANICS DO-IT-YOURSELF ENCYCLOPEDIA. If so, when Volume II arrives, simply remit the low subscriber price of only $5.95 plus a small charge for shipping & handling and any applicable sales tax.

Then, the remaining volumes will be sent to you over a five-month period -- <u>each shipment strictly "on approval."</u> Pay for each volume (one payment a month) at the low subscriber price of only $5.95 -- or return it within the 14-day Free-Examination Period and owe nothing.

BUY AS FEW OR AS MANY VOLUMES AS YOU WISH. CANCEL ANY TIME!

Remember -- Volume I of the POPULAR MECHANICS DO-IT-YOURSELF ENCYCLOPEDIA is your "Free Sample" -- yours to keep even if you decide <u>not</u> to buy anything.

But to get it, you have to sign and mail the enclosed Reply Card.

Do it <u>today</u>.

Cordially,

J. Michael Walters
For POPULAR MECHANICS

P.S. If you take pride in work well done, want to give your family the better things in life...then you need POPULAR MECHANICS <u>how-to-do-it</u> information on AIR CONDITIONERS... BARBECUES...BOATS...BIRDHOUSES...BOOKCASES... BURGLAR ALARMS...CAULKING...CAMERAS...

CONCRETE...CLOCKS...DOORS...DRILL PRESSES...
ENGINES...FAUCETS...FENCES...GUNS...GETTING IN
SHAPE...HEATERS...INSULATION...KITCHENS...
KITS...LANDSCAPING...METALWORKING...
OUTBOARDS...PAINTING...PLUMBING...PLYWOOD...
REMODELING...ROOFS...RAIN GUTTERS...SEPTIC
TANKS...SEWING CENTERS...SKIN DIVING...SOLAR
ENERGY...SWIMMING POOLS...TILE...TOOLS...
TOYS...TRAILERS...TREES...UPHOLSTERY...
VACATION HOMES...VACUUMS...WINDOWS...
WOODWORKING. These are just a few of the
subjects covered in the 20-volume POPULAR
MECHANICS DO-IT-YOURSELF ENCYCLOPEDIA. And
Volume I is yours to keep -- but only if you
mail the Reply Card NOW!

Our Promise

When Popular Mechanics says <u>free</u>, it really
means <u>free</u>. Unlike some of those book and
record club deals that promise something
special at the beginning, and then commit you
to expensive purchases later on in the fine
print, this free offer does not obligate you
in <u>any</u> way. This is not a book club. You'll
receive your free book with no obligation --
ever -- to accept anything else.

This might be my favorite letter of the six I'm reprinting for you here. It's anti-establishment, has a slightly angry, us-against-the-world tone. And is clearly written for guys who like to fix and build things themselves, guys who get a giddy, tingly feeling when they have a hammer or power saw in their hand.

If you understand your reader, you are 90 percent of the way to writing an effective sales letter. I can't imagine many women answering this letter, except maybe on behalf of her husband if he's the roll-up-his-sleeves and get-his-hands-dirty handyman type.

This is actually more of a lead-generation letter. *Popular Mechanics* is willing to invest a significant sum of money to find its buyers—giving away an expensively-produced free book and backing-up the offer with an attention-getting guarantee. If you are a do-it-

204 How To Write...

yourself-guy, I can't imagine turning down this impressive offer.

Clearly, *Popular Mechanics* is convinced of the value of this product, as it's counting on the strength of the free sample to sell the rest of the encyclopedia set and to create loyal customers for its magazine and vast array of do-it-yourself books and manuals. *Popular Mechanics* knows the average long-term value of a customer, and therefore how much it can afford to invest to acquire a new customer.

Note also the double use of the "Johnson Box"—at the start, and then again at the close of the letter—which summarizes the offer and restates the impressive guarantee.

* * * *

American Express

Dear Mr. Masterson:

Quite frankly, the American Express Card is not for everyone. And not everyone who applies for Card membership is approved.

However, because we believe you will benefit from Card Membership, I've enclosed a special invitation for you to apply for the most honored and prestigious financial instrument available to people who travel, vacation, and entertain.

The American Express Card is the perfect example of the old adage, "You get what you pay for."

For example, you get a truly impressive array of extra privileges, all designed for your convenience and security:

- A Worldwide Network of Travel Service Offices* is at your Service. Enjoy personal attention at any of the nearby 1,000 American Express Offices -- Your "homes away from home" -- around the globe.

- Cash your Personal Check at Thousands of Locations. Cash up to $250 at participating hotels and motels, and up to $1,000 at most American Express Travel Services Offices all over the world. (Subject to cash availability and local regulations.)

- Card Lost or Stolen? You'll Get a Quick Replacement. If the Card is lost or stolen, an emergency replacement will be provided at any Travel Service Office in the world, usually by the end of the next business day.

- Obtain Emergency Funds Instantly. Once you've enrolled in this convenient service, our network of automated Travelers Cheque Dispensers lets you obtain up to $500...in 60 seconds or less!

- Carry $100,000 of Travel Accident Insurance. Just charge your tickets to the Card, and you, your spouse or dependent children under the age of 23 are automatically covered when traveling by common carrier on land, sea, or in the air. It's underwritten by Fireman's Fund Insurance Companies, San Rafael, California, for approximately 35 cents of the annual Card Membership fee.

- Your Hotel Reservations are Assured. As an American Express Card Member, if you request, your hotel room will be held for you until checkout the following day at nearly 8,000 participating hotels.

- Enjoy Special Express Hotel Service. Speedy check-in and checkout is available to Card Members at more than 1,000 hotels, including Hilton, Hyatt, Marriott, Sheraton, and more.

Extras like these only begin to tell the story of

How To Write...

American Express Card security, emergency protection, and convenience. You'll also enjoy:

- <u>Unequalled Mobility</u>. The Card is welcomed by the world's major airlines, car rental agencies, railroads, and cruise lines. Plus it pays for auto parts and servicing at thousands of locations nationwide.

- <u>A Worldwide Welcome</u>. Fine restaurants, hotel resorts, and a host of other establishments around this world, and right in your hometown, recognize the Card and welcome your patronage.

- <u>Purchasing Power</u>. No need to carry large amounts of cash. The Card takes care of shopping needs, whether you're choosing a wardrobe, buying theater tickets, sending flowers, or hosting a dinner (even if you can't be there!)

- <u>Financial Freedom</u>. Unlike bank cards, the American Express Card imposes no pre-set spending limit. Purchases are approved based on your ability to pay as demonstrated by your past spending, payment patterns, and personal resources. So you are free to make your own decisions about when and where to use the Card.

In a few words, American Express Card Membership is the most effective letter of introduction to the world of travel, entertainment, and the good life yet devised. Yet surprisingly, these benefits are all yours to enjoy for the modest fee of just $35 a year.

Why not apply for Card Membership today? All you have to do is fill out and mail the enclosed application. As soon as it is approved, we'll send along the Card, without delay.

```
                    Sincerely,


                    Diane Shalb
                    Vice President

P.S.  Apply today, and enjoy all the benefits of
      Card Membership. Those listed here are just a
      handful of what's available. A full listing is
      included in the Guide to Card Member Services
      you'll receive along with the Card.
```

This is the offer that built American Express. You've probably received one (or many) of these letters. The letter relies on one of the most powerful human desires—the desire for status.

People want to be members of an exclusive club. Possession of the card tells those who see it that you've made it in life, that you're successful, that you are good enough to be in this exclusive club. This card shows the world that you are a cut above most. At least, that's what American Express wants us to believe.

Plus, American Express delivers a menu of attractive benefits and conveniences, mostly aimed at appealing to the desire many have to be pampered. "Privileges" is the word the letter uses. In addition, the letter taps into our fears and anxieties by promising to be there for us in times of emergency.

Notice also that this letter is personalized—essential if your offer relies on an argument built around the honor of receiving such an invitation. This letter is a superb example of how a short letter can pack a powerful punch. In this case, gilding the lily with a long letter would undermine the prestige of the invitation.

The tone of the letter is arrogant and elitist. "We don't need to sell you," the letter implies. "You should feel honored by this invitation." This letter is really more of an announcement than an invitation. The tone suggests there's no possibility that any right-thinking person would refuse to join if invited. In fact, this letter is really just an invitation to *apply* for membership. We're supposed to feel honored to be invited just to apply. This is an offer built on snob appeal and the desire for status.

Think about how you might make an offer along these lines to your very best clients and customers—your VIP list? Everyone wants to be treated like a VIP.

Prevention

Emmaus, PA 18099

Dear Reader:

My Grandmother lived with us when I was growing up.

She used to give me chamomile tea when my stomach was upset. She insisted that the family use vinegar to rinse hair and made a cucumber cleanser for my face. As I grew older, I decided Grandmother was hopelessly out of date.

Then a few years ago, I began remembering how it was when I lived with her. How shiny and healthy our hair had always been. How beautiful my skin remained throughout adolescence. How full of energy and vitality all of us were without our soft drinks, candies and snack foods (she wouldn't allow them in the house -- "empty foods," she'd snort...and hand me a box of raisins or dried apricots).

I was reminded of grandmother when I noticed how often the government removed a chemical from the market after everyone had been eating it for years. I began wondering whether the products I was using today would be forbidden tomorrow.

And that started me thinking about how many chemicals I used and ate. Almost everything contains chemicals! I kept reading how scientists thought some of them caused serious medical problems. How simple things like headache remedies could create other troubles.

I was stunned by the number of foods that were almost completely "fake" -- most of the good things had been taken out and chemical substitutes put in.
You read about threats and dangers to your health like these everyday in almost every newspaper and magazine you open.

But I know of only one publication that tells you --
sincerely and consistently -- how you may combat these
problems...what you may do to try to live healthier in
this often unhealthy world of ours: PREVENTION
magazine.

If you've ever seen PREVENTION, you know its
style. Understandable. Practical. Down-to-Earth.
It's the magazine that over two million Americans
regularly turn to for the help and advice that they
cannot find from any other source -- sometimes
doctors included.

If you haven't seen the magazine...I'd like to
send you the latest issue so you can take a good
look. I'm sure you'll find its "feel better" ideas
as stimulating as a breath of fresh air.

To get your no-risk, no obligation copy of
PREVENTION magazine...

1. Just mail the enclosed postpaid card. BUT
   SPEND NO MONEY NOW.

2. We'll send you PREVENTION and enter a trial
   no-risk 12-month subscription in your name.

3. If you like what you see and want to subscribe
   to PREVENTION magazine's unique brand of "feed
   better" advice, simply pay the $8.99 invoice.

If not, just mark "cancel" on our bill, return it
and owe nothing. You keep the first issue free of
charge.

Now, that's a fair offer, isn't it?

And we're making it so easy because we want you
to take just one look -- so you can see just how
valuable PREVENTION magazine may be in your life.
Why so valuable?

Because PREVENTION is the cheapest, most easily
accessible source that you have to much of the

latest medical research findings...to some of the alternative ways to try to "get better" and "stay better" without resorting to drugs and surgery...to the basic, earthy, natural approach to better living that my Grandmother (and perhaps, <u>yours</u>, too) knew almost intuitively.

WHY DO YOU NEED PREVENTION?

It's an honest question. And, basically, the answer is three-fold:

1. <u>PREVENTION tries to help you even out the increasing odds against your better health</u>.

Open any newspaper or magazine and you're likely to read about another chemical in your environment... another additive in your food...another way that may shorten your life span; another way perhaps leading to diseases like cancer or heart trouble.

It's getting so depressing that many people block it out of their minds. They "grow accustomed" to the new dangers. They try to pretend they don't exist. But that doesn't make these potential dangers disappear; it doesn't make life any healthier, longer...or even happier.

PREVENTION tries to alert you to the dangers, too. But we can't stop them. Every issue tells you what you may do to try to avoid them...possibly correct them...and, in some cases, even perhaps repair some of the damage that they may have already done.

2. <u>PREVENTION tells you more than your doctor perhaps can or will</u>.

Today, surgery and drugs are not the only "get better" alternatives available to you. There are other options open. Options that, often, are safer, cheaper, gentler than those of "traditional medicine." Time after time, we've found that a number of today's physicians may not even be aware of these alternatives.

So how can you expect to know of them?

PREVENTION tries to be your link. You learn about how your body functions...what it needs for better well-being...how you may, many times, correct a minor illness or ailment yourself. PREVENTION may help you be a more intelligent, more aware medical consumer. (After all, your health is your responsibility.)

3. PREVENTION seems to work well. The PREVENTION System for Better Health apparently gets results.

If it did not, we would most certainly not be the number one health magazine in the world today -- which we are -- with over two million regular subscribers.

We make no miracle claims; offer no instant result. All we say is if you truly want better health...

...if you want to try to live a longer, more active life...if you want to treat what may be the source -- not symptoms alone -- of your health problems...if you want to know more about what you may do to live healthier in this unhealthy world of ours...

...PREVENTION may show you -- step by step -- the things that you may do to help achieve these desires.

Isn't it worth a free look? And if PREVENTION works for you, isn't it well worth the $6.99 subscription price? We think so. Over two million monthly readers think so.

But what do you think? Look first (at our risk) and then decide.

Here's how...

REMEMBER OUR NO-RISK OFFER: LOOK NOW, DECIDE TO SUBSCRIBE LATER.

How To Write...

Of course, I could go on and on about PREVENTION. Sharing with you the many ways the PREVENTION System has helped me personally...telling you about specific natural healing techniques...quoting some moving testimony from PREVENTION readers...

...but I'll spare your time.

One free look is worth a thousand words of advertising. And PREVENTION speaks for itself -- <u>POWERFULLY</u>.

So you be the judge.

Just mail the enclosed card to inspect PREVENTION -- the modern "get better, feel better," natural health system whose roots go very deep indeed.

I'm on the PREVENTION System. And I've got to tell you, I feel better -- and look better -- because of it. It has helped me. It may help you too.

I hope you try PREVENTION. I hope everybody does. We need a little more "real" in our lives and a few less substitutes.

              Sincerely,

              Sandy Gibb

P.S.   <u>ACT NOW AND GET A FREE BOOK ABOUT THE PREVENTION SYSTEM</u>! For all those who mail the enclosed card...

       ...We have a free bonus: a copy of the PREVENTION SYSTEM FOR BETTER HEALTH -- the book that explains in plain language how this natural health method works. Here are the basics of the 35-year-old system that has helped improve the well-being of so many over the years.

       You can't buy a copy of this remarkable book anywhere. But it's yours free -- whether you

subscribe to the magazine or not -- so take
action now, while you're thinking about it.

P.P.S. AN EXTRA FREE BOOKLET...AND ADDED SAVINGS!

If you're planning to give PREVENTION a try,
why not try 24-months? There are plenty of
good reasons why you should.

1. THERE'S NO EXTRA RISK. Our money-back on
unmailed copies privilege assures it.

2. GUARD AGAINST PRICE INCREASES. They're
almost inevitable with our present economy.
Buying a 24-month subscription could be an
insurance policy against highest pries.

3. GET THIS BOOK AS A BONUS. In addition to
your free copy of THE PREVENTION SYSTEM FOR
BETTER HEALTH, we'll send you a copy of our
HERBS FOR HEALTH when you subscribe for 24
months.

Now you can get acquainted with one of the alternatives
to drugs and medications: the healing herbs. Here are
the "medicines of yesterday" that are making a comeback.
You'll find herbal treatments and folk "remedies" for
dozens of common ailments. And you'll learn to know and
use 70 wonderful plants and herbs in HERBS FOR HEALTH.
You can't buy it anywhere, but it's yours free from
PREVENTION with this trial subscription.

Here's another letter that begins with a story—this one about the
letter-signer's grandmother. The letter uses nostalgia—a desire to
return to simpler and perhaps happier times of old—as a way to put us
into a buying frame of mind. And the letter taps into the most
powerful motive driving people to buy—fear. In this case, fear of all
the chemicals (poisons) companies put into our foods, in addition to all
the healthy ingredients companies strip out of our foods.
And this letter makes a strong argument for many of the old-time
remedies that worked so well for many ailments and
illnesses—remedies our grandmothers knew, but that have been
forgotten by modern medicine, but also which are coming back into

vogue because they are effective.

Similar to the *Popular Mechanics* and *Newsweek* letters reprinted earlier, this letter is folksy, conversational and very easy to read.

You'll see the kinds of grammatical errors you hear in regular face-to-face conversations. The writer is perfectly capable of using proper grammar that would pass muster in a college writing course, but chooses not to in order to capture the casual style of someone sitting across your kitchen table having a conversation.

More rigorous use of correct grammar would be important for another audience—perhaps when writing to college-educated corporate executives or to English professors—but not here. The writer is not trying to impress a college English professor. This writer is talking to average folks who are worried about their health and who suspect there's something wrong with many of the processed foods we buy at the grocery store. *Prevention's* two million subscribers attest to the success of this approach.

Notice also that the P.S. is packed with special bonuses. Books and special reports that can't be found anywhere else, and that are exactly in line with the subject of the main product offered, are proven response-boosting devices. Many readers will make the decision to subscribe to the magazine just to get the valuable bonuses.

I love the understated tone of this famous sales letter for the *Kiplinger Washington Letter*, the best selling financial advice newsletter of all time.

The Kiplinger Washington Editors, Inc.

1729 H Street, Northwest, Washington, D.C. 2006 Telephone: 202.887.6400

More Growth and Inflation Ahead...
and what you can do about it.

The next few years will see business climb to the
highest level this country has ever known. And with
it...inflation.

This combination may be hard for you to accept
under today's conditions. But the fact remains
that those who do prepare for both inflation AND
growth ahead will reap big dividends for their
foresight, and avoid the blunders others will make.

You'll get the information you need for this type
of planning in the Kiplinger Washington Letter...and
the enclosed form will bring you the next 26 issues
of this helpful service on a "Try-out" basis. The
fee: Less than 81 cents per week...only $21 for the
six months...and tax-deductible for business or
investment purposes.

During the depression, in 1935, the Kiplinger
Washington Letter warned of inflation and told what
to do about it. Those who heeded its advice were
ready when prices began to rise.

Again, in January of 1946, the Letter renounced the
widely-held view that a severe post-war depression was
inevitable. Instead, it predicted shortages, rising
wages and prices, a high level of business. And
again, those who heeded its advice were able to
avoid losses, to cash in on the surging economy of
the late '40s, early '50s and mid-'60s. It then
kept its clients prepared for the swings of the
'70s, keeping them a step ahead each time.

Now Kiplinger not only foresees expansion ahead,
but also continuing inflation, and in this weekly
Letter to clients, he points out profit opportunities
in the future...and also dangers.

How To Write...

The Kiplinger Letter not only keeps you informed of present trends and developments, but also gives you advance notice on the sort & long-range business outlook...inflation forecasts...energy predictions... housing...federal legislative prospects...politics... investment trends & pointers ...tax outlook and advice...labor, wage settlement prospects...upcoming gov't rules & regulations...ANYTHING that will have an effect on your business, your personal finances, your family.

To take advantage of this opportunity to try the Letter and benefit from its keen judgments and helpful advice during the fast-changing months ahead...fill in and return the form with your $21 payment. And do it with this guarantee: That you may cancel the service and get a prompt refund of the unused part of your payment any time you feel it is not worth far more to you than it costs.

I'll start your service as soon as I hear from you, and you'll have each weekly issue on your desk every Monday morning thereafter.

       Sincerely,

       Stanley Mayes
       Assistant to the President

SAM:kga

P.S.   More than half of all new subscribers sign up for a full year at $42. In appreciation, we'll send you FREE five special Kiplinger Reports on receipt of your payment when you take a full year's service, too. Details are spelled out on the enclosed slip. Same money-back guarantee and tax-deductibility apply.

This letter is simple, to-the-point and uses several proven motivators to persuade its readers to buy: <u>fear</u> of inflation and <u>fear</u> of missing important information that may cost the reader money; plus the possibility that the *Kiplinger Letter* will give the reader a financial edge (greed). <u>Fear</u> is the #1 motivation driving people to buy, and <u>greed</u> is probably #2. Put those two motivations (incentives) together, and you have a powerful selling formula.

In addition, the *Kiplinger Letter* is inexpensive. As such, this offer is difficult to pass up if you are at all interested in your financial well-being (most of us are).

This offer would appeal to subscribers to the *Wall Street Journal*, *Forbes* magazine and other publications covering personal finance. This sales letter also outlines Kiplinger's impressive track-record, dating back to the 1930s, of giving financial advice that proved to be on target. *The Kiplinger Letter* is among the most successful and widely circulated financial newsletters ever published. This sales letter is certainly worthy of careful study.

The Lesson: If you want to learn golf, copy Tiger Woods. Study what he does. And learn *why* he does what he does. And then practice. If you want to write great sales letters, study the six great sales letters I've reprinted here. And then practice.

Whether you are writing to a few people or a million people, if you follow the approach of these six of the greatest sales letters ever written, you are well on your way to near limitless success.

Chapter Eighty
A closing word

The difference between a sales letter and Madison Avenue advertising is this:

Unlike your sales letter, the major corporate 60-second advertisements you see on TV are not aimed at generating immediate sales and inquiries. And they don't. There are no results to measure for the Madison Avenue ad.

These ads are designed to create brand recognition and public awareness. They are aimed at making the public familiar with the brand and the name of the product.

How To Write...

There is no real way to precisely measure the effectiveness of these Madison Avenue ads. The big corporations know they must advertise. And they are just left hoping their ads are successful. But there's no real benchmark for success, other than the decision-makers at the corporation signing off on the big ad buy.

We certainly know these ads are successful for the ad agency, some of which are racking up billions of dollars in billings. But we have no precise way of knowing if these ads are successful for the client...because no orders or inquiries are arriving at the office in answer to these ads.

In this sense, the Madison Avenue ad agency's primary mission in life is not to create ads that win customers, but to create ads that impress the corporate client. If the ad happens to be good and brings customers in, that's a bonus for the ad agency. But who will ever know if that's what's happening?

The primary mission of the Madison Avenue ad agency is to sell the client on the ad campaign, not to create ads that actually sell product.

Who really knows how all those Nike ads are doing?

The ads are attention-getting and interesting. They have certainly done a great job of creating brand awareness and a hip image for the company. I certainly enjoy the Nike ads. No doubt the ads are doing well for Nike and are helping Nike build its image around the world. But Nike has no way of knowing how each individual ad is doing. Nike has no idea how many sales each individual ad is generating. Nike really has no way of knowing its "return on investment" for each ad launched.

The best Nike can do is guess. The best Nike can do is ASSUME its ads are effective.

But even if Nike's "building brand awareness" and image advertising method is working well for Nike, there's very little any of us can learn from this approach. There's no model here for the entrepreneur to follow.

"Go out and just copy Nike" would be silly advice for you because you don't have a multi-billion dollar advertising budget.

It would cost you hundreds of millions, more likely billions, of dollars in advertising to create an image and a "general public awareness" of you, your company, your brand, or your product.

Then you would need to have in place a massive manufacturing infrastructure and a nationwide distribution network to make sure your product is available everywhere.

It would be enormously costly for you to follow the Nike "build brand awareness" and image strategy even in the smallest of local markets. The production of these TV ads alone is a major undertaking.

This big corporate approach is of zero use to you or me. If it were, you would not have gotten this far in this book.

The other approach is to sell people our products and services in one-on-one personal conversations.

That's what salesmen do. This is how the rest of us, who don't have a billion dollar advertising budget, must make our living.

But since the salesman cannot be everywhere at once making his one-on-one presentations to prospective customers, the next best thing is the sales letter.

Used properly, the sales letter is the salesman's most powerful tool. The sales letter, for much less cost than a personal one-on-one meeting, seeks to start a conversation with your prospect with the aim of selling your product or service.

Sometimes you can sell the product on the strength of the letter alone. Sometimes, for high-priced products and services, you just want to find out if there's interest in what you are selling—that is, you are seeking to generate qualified leads. Either way, the goal of your mailing is clear and the results are precisely measurable.

Remember, if your marketing is not exactly and precisely measurable, it's really not marketing, it's PR.

The Madison Avenue ads are PR. This book is about true marketing—that is, showing you how to produce results that are precisely measurable.

That's the difference between the sales letter, and the image advertising that Nike is doing.

Performed correctly, you should know to the penny how much it costs you to generate a sale. The mission of the sales letter is not to create a general awareness of your brand or your product. The one and only purpose of your letter is to sell.

One of the great features of the sales letter is its near infinite flexibility and versatility. You can use it to reach one person or a million people. Unlike the Madison Avenue ads, the sales letter is not one-size-fits-all carpet-bomb advertising.

The sales letter allows you to target your most likely buyers with laser-like precision. The sales letter is the opposite of broadcasting; it's the narrowest of "narrow-casting." And it's advertising that can pay for itself almost immediately with the orders that come back in answer to your mailings.

If a Madison Avenue-style ad campaign is like a nuclear bomb that hits everyone in an area, a direct mail marketing campaign is more like precision surgery. That's why direct mail is still the most cost-effective advertising there is.

As I'm writing these words, I happen to be attending an Internet marketing conference. When I tell my fellow conference participants I'm an old-fashioned direct mail marketing specialist, I can see them begin to yawn. These young Internet pioneers, most of them in their 20s, are very nice and polite, but they see me as a dinosaur. To these kids, there is no other media.

They don't seem to know that not everyone wants to sit all day at their computers. People will continue to want to go to shopping malls. People still want to talk face-to-face with a salesman. People are still reading their newspapers. And people still go to their mailboxes (their postal mailboxes) everyday to pick up their mail, sort through it and read what grabs their attention, just as our parents, grandparents, and great-grandparents did. This will not change in any of our lifetimes.

The Internet will not replace the mailman anymore than the telephone replaced the mailman. Radio did not replace newspapers and TV did not replace radio. Movies have not replaced books. People continue to buy books, which have been around for thousands of years. All these media continue to do just fine. The Internet is just one more communications channel, one more medium, and one more tool the marketer must learn to master— one that has advantages as well as disadvantages.

Don't get me wrong. I love the Internet. I'm spending a great deal of time learning everything I can about Internet marketing. The Internet today is an absolutely essential marketing tool, as is a toll-free 1.800 number. I remember the "infomercial" mania. I was told the infomercial would put us direct mail marketers out of business. Now the infomercial mania has died down. But good old-fashioned direct mail continues to gather strength.

According to the Direct Marketing Association, nearly $60 billion a year is now spent on direct mail marketing, and spending on direct mail marketing is rising at about six percent annually.

One reason direct mail continues to grow is that it's not limited to 60 seconds or less as on radio and TV, one- or two-page presentations as in magazine ads, a computer screen as on the Web, a boring format readers can delete with one key stroke as in email, or one color as for a fax. Nor does direct mail require an enormous budget, as is needed with the infomercial or any TV ad campaign.

Direct mail cannot be blocked with caller ID or other screening devices for telemarketing. And, unlike with telemarketing and email (spam) we don't have to worry about Congress passing any laws to stop or hinder our mailings so long as the government is in the mail delivery business.

With direct mail you can have any number of inserts. You can use all the colors you want. And there are an almost unlimited number of formats you can deploy to grab and hold the attention of your reader. You can use foldouts, pop-ups, and even enclose computer disks, books, and CDs. You can put your letters and enclosures in boxes, tubes, or plastic bags to grab the attention of your reader.

In direct mail you are limited only by your imagination and economics of the project.

There was a day when many marketing experts, including large advertising agencies, believed that direct mail was only suitable for selling $10, $20, and $50 consumer items. Direct mail, they thought, was useful for magazine subscriptions, book clubs, kitchen gadgets, and to solicit small $10 and $15 donations for charities, not much more.

Today I buy Omaha steaks, gourmet Gevalia coffee, and clothes through the mail. I bought my most recent car through the mail, a shiny black Audi A-6. I needed a new car. A sophisticated direct marketer knew that the lease on my current car was about to expire, and knew that I would soon need a new car. A direct mail piece arrived at my home offering me a brand new Audi for much less than my local Audi dealer. The mailing promised I would pay the exact amount for the car offered in the mail piece—not a penny more.

This promise got my attention. When is the price of a car ever actually the price advertised? I got on the phone, asked some questions to make sure I would be getting the exact car advertised in the mailing. And, sure enough, that was the price. Within 24 hours, the car was delivered to my home, like a pizza!

I signed the papers. If I wasn't satisfied, I could return the car within 10 days and owe nothing. No long waits at the dealer. No being held hostage for hours by an aggressive salesman trying to sell me the undercoating or extra service warranty I didn't need or want. No hassles. Instead, I had been offered and I had purchased an Audi via direct mail—a $48,000 item.

Not only is direct mail still by far the most powerful and cost-effective medium for building your customer base, direct mail is absolutely essential for maintaining the customer bases created by the Internet and all the other new media.

Not long ago, Fortune 500 companies scoffed at direct mail as junk mail. But now more than half of the Fortune 500 corporations have opened up massive direct mail marketing operations.

General Foods, Procter & Gamble, IBM, Dell, Compaq, Apple, AOL, Nieman Marcus, Nordstrom, Bloomingdale's, Visa, MasterCard, American Express, America's biggest banks and financial institutions, jewelers, realtors, airlines, hotels, and automobile companies are all now marketing heavily to consumers through the mail.

Why?

Because they know they must use the mail to win the battle for market share; and because these huge companies see how well direct mail works. The results are measurable and predictable. They can see a return on investment.

Summing Up

If you remember nothing else you've read in this entire book, I urge you to remember these nine points:

1) Write about what your reader wants, not about what you want.

2) You can succeed if you write a poor letter for the right list, but the best letter in the world cannot work to the wrong list.

3) Craft headlines and sub-headlines that will grab the interest of your reader.

4) Persuade your reader with facts and reasons, not fantastic claims and empty hype.

5) Keep your reader's interest with fascinating details and narrative (like Stephen King) that make it easier to keep reading than to skip what you have to say.

6) Craft an offer no intelligent reader can pass up.

7) Don't make your guarantee a boring after-thought, but instead create a super-charged guarantee that will catch your reader's attention, like Nordstrom's famous guarantee.

8) Give your reader good, solid, credible reasons for answering your letter today, not tomorrow.

9) Make sure your letter reads like a personal letter from one person to another, that it does not come across as mass – advertising—even if economics dictate that you must mail a cheap non-personalized "Dear Friend" letter.

Whether you are writing to a few people or a million people, if you achieve these nine things, you will succeed.

If I can be of further assistance to you in your marketing efforts, please feel free to send me an email at:

lovesdirectmail@aol.com

...or visit my Web site at:

www.DirectMailCopywriters.com

I would be happy to answer any further questions you might have concerning the marketing challenges you're facing.

Sincerely,

Ben

Ben Hart
DirectMailCopywriters.com

P.S. Check out **DirectMarketingInstitute.com** for the <u>Target</u>

<u>Marketing Boot Camp schedule</u> for entrepreneurs.

Target Marketing Boot Camps take place throughout the year and are no longer just about direct mail. They now cover all areas of direct marketing, including the Internet. I hope to see you at the next one.

I'd also very much like to get your feedback on this book. Was it helpful to you? Please send me your comments at **lovesdirectmail@aol.com**

Some good reasons not to put this book aside before you've made sure you're on my mailing list.

Dear Motivated Entrepreneur,

I would love to keep you informed about...

- ✓ The books I'm writing that will help you improve your marketing;

- ✓ The Target Marketing Boot Camps, Seminars and Workshops I'm holding; and

- ✓ New marketing breakthroughs I'm discovering nearly every day that might be just what you need to catapult your business and sales to the next level.

In addition, I have a brand new book out called *Automatic Marketing* that might interest you.

This book is all about how to use 21st Century technologies (as well as old fashioned 20th Century technologies) and strategies to make almost all your marketing automatic, robotic and hands-free...

...so that you never need to make another sales call, while your business grows explosively and exponentially, on its own, even while you play golf or sleep.

This is a book that should interest every entrepreneur.

Or you might like to start receiving the **Direct Marketing Intelligence Letter,** in which I will report to you what's working well right now in direct marketing.

How To Write...

Plus, I'm holding periodic teleseminars and webinars I'd like to alert you to, where you can hear from some of the world's greatest direct marketers.

And there's so much more in the field of marketing I'd like to make you aware of, as soon as I learn about it.

That's what's so great about this field called direct marketing.

You can never learn it all.

I learn something new about direct marketing almost every day, and I'd like to have you on my mailing list so I can tell you about my latest marketing discoveries.

Just send me an email with all your contact information, and I'll be glad to add you to my list of marketing enthusiasts.

Again, my email address is:

lovesdirectmail@aol.com

When you send me your contact information, be sure you give me the email address you always use, not the email address for your junk mail. And give me your real name, not a fake name.

Some of my readers think they are very clever when they give me junk contact information about themselves.

But these people are always missing some very important, time-sensitive information.

For example, I often hold impromptu teleseminars and conference call briefings with only a few hours of advance notice.

So be sure to give me your best contact information -- the same contact information your friends and relatives have on you.

Don't worry, I won't abuse this privilege.

And I won't fill up your email and postal mailboxes with spam and junk.

I'll only send you good information periodically on how to make your marketing more successful.

I look forward to getting to know you better.

Happy Marketing!

Ben

Ben Hart
DirectMailCopywriters.com

P.S. You can also call my toll-free number to leave give me your contact information. The number is **800.599.5150.**

P.P.S. And read this last letter again to see if you can spot many of the rules, principles and precepts for writing effective marketing letters that I've been describing to you in this book. <u>Hint</u>: This is a classic "lead generation" letter.

How To Write...

Notes

Printed in the United States
42880LVS00006B/127-288